Evelyn V. Brunson, Ed.D.

College of Education
University of North Florida

THE PROFESSIONAL SECRETARY

PRENTICE-HALL, INC., Englewood Cliffs, New Jersey

Library of Congress Cataloging in Publication Data

Brunson, Evelyn
    The professional secretary.

    1. Secretaries — Handbooks, manuals, etc.   I. Title.
HF5547.5.B78   651'.3741   73–12083
ISBN   0–13–725887–9
ISBN   0–13–725903–4 (pbk.)

TO DIXIE AND DREW

10   9   8   7   6   5   4   3   2

Printed in the United States of America

PRENTICE-HALL INTERNATIONAL, INC., *London*
PRENTICE-HALL OF AUSTRALIA, PTY. LTD., *Sydney*
PRENTICE-HALL OF CANADA, LTD., *Toronto*
PRENTICE-HALL OF INDIA PRIVATE LTD., *New Delhi*
PRENTICE-HALL OF JAPAN, INC., *Tokyo*

PART ONE

1

THE SECRETARIAL POSITION   1

2

THE INTERVIEW   15

Contents

3

4

5

6

7

DEVELOP GOOD WORK HABITS 113

8

THE ART OF DICTATION 133

9

CHANGING CAREERS OF THE FUTURE 147

10

THE WHOLE SECRETARY 157

PART TWO

THE PROFESSIONAL SECRETARY'S REFERENCE MANUAL 163

The Professional Secretary has been prepared as a finishing course for the aspiring professional secretary. I believe that it can be used with equal success by the teacher or by the executive in the process of job performance evaluation.

As the names of the chapters indicate, topics suggested by day-to-day office routine are examined. Areas of secretarial responsibility that have rarely been explored in depth are discussed, and emphasis is placed on cause and effect and the secretary's relationship to various office situations. I have made a definite effort to relate previously completed academic studies to actual situations in order to help the secretary understand the office role, but I have avoided dwelling on subject matter rightfully contained in other courses.

The approach is to recognize a problem, raise questions, and discuss various approaches to finding a solution. The secretarial student is encouraged to think about the job, the responsibilities, the actions and the reactions of people in various situations. As the student gains understanding, he is encouraged to develop initiative based on creative thinking, and thereby show professional improvement in the ability to relate to all facets of the secretarial job.

This textbook may be used in a reference capacity by businessmen. There are subjects that are difficult or awkward to discuss with employees. With access to a reference book, the employer can hold in-service training sessions with the secretary in

Preface

conjunction with employment evaluation and improved job performance.

The teacher of Secretarial Procedures will find this book a different but challenging way of presenting material the secretarial student needs. Skills that are taught in the managerial area of a business administration program are becoming necessary in the secretarial program, and they must be adapted to meet the needs of the secretary. These skills include the use of time and motion studies to increase efficiency in the secretary's working schedule, the introduction of proper techniques of interviewing, and building a good working relationship with boss and peers.

The material requires the use of innovative teaching techniques; I have provided suggested projects sections to assist in the book's use as a text, and I have prepared a teacher's manual to indicate various approaches to presenting the material. The dynamic teacher will find additional ways of building learning situations based on or related to the text. Proper use of this textbook will provide an educational experience that can increase the student's versatility, prepare him to cope with rapid and constant change, and develop his ability to judge between the significant and the transitory. The book includes many examples that urge the student to solve problems involving understanding of the material presented in the text. The cartoon illustrations are designed to make a specific point or to emphasize a certain idea.

The style of the book has been kept simple so as not to interfere with the ideas presented.

The author expresses appreciation to all those who contributed experiences that aided in the preparation of this book. Secretaries, businessmen, professors, and students have reviewed the manuscript and offered observations and suggestions that have made this book a more practical tool with which to approach secretarial education. I wish to express special appreciation to my family who, by virtue of accepting their roles of responsibility in family life, have given me the extra time needed for the preparation of this material.

Evelyn Brunson
Jacksonville, Florida

Code of Ethics

Recognizing the secretary's position of trust, we resolve in all of our activities to be guided by the highest ideals for which THE NATIONAL SECRETARIES ASSOCIATION stands, to establish, practice, and promote professional standards; and to be ethical and understanding in all of our business associations.

We resolve to promote the interest of the business in which we are employed; to exemplify loyalty and conscientiousness at all times; and to maintain dignity and poise under all circumstances.

We further resolve to share knowledge; to encourage ambition and inspire hope; and to sustain faith, knowing that the eternal laws of God are the ultimate laws under which we may truly succeed.

Courtesy of
THE NATIONAL SECRETARIES ASSOCIATION
INTERNATIONAL

A Secretary's Credo

I BELIEVE THAT . . . the philosophy of the secretarial profession embodies a foundation of logic and learning, ethics and integrity, courtesy and understanding, and a desire to be of benefit to others;

. . . the principal obligation of a secretary is to function as a support to management and to increase the effectiveness of the executive;

. . . a secretary occupies a position of confidence, trust, and responsibility and accepts this position as a privilege to guard carefully;

. . . secretarial excellence requires comprehensive educational preparation;

. . . a secretary strives for self-improvement through a program of continuing education;

. . . the maintenance of high standards is essential to the continuing advancement of the secretarial profession;

. . . the qualifications of a secretary are enhanced by a business-like demeanor and by friendliness, cooperation, good humor, and enthusiasm;

. . . a secretary should assume responsibility for guiding qualified young people toward secretarial careers;

. . . a secretarial career is both challenging and rewarding;

SO BELIEVING . . . I THEREFORE dedicate myself to preserve and to practice these principles and to uphold them at all times with dignity and honor.

Courtesy of
THE NATIONAL SECRETARIES ASSOCIATION INTERNATIONAL

1

The Secretarial Position

The secretarial position is full of possibilities. Can you imagine any other occupation that is called for in every phase of the working world? The secretarial profession is usually thought of in relation to business and industry; but in addition to the commonly defined business offices, business and industry include fashion design, accounting, politics, travel bureaus, foreign service, social bureaus, news bureaus, courts, and many other aspects. All the secretary need do is to sort through all the professions of business and industry to determine the most desirable one for personal interest and personal future goals.

The Open Door

There is an additional advantage to the secretarial position that you may have overlooked — the secretarial field is very often an open door into another type of profession. For example, an aspiring model might do well to practice her secretarial skills in the offices of a model agency, where she can make contacts leading to a modeling job when she is ready. An aspiring actress might accept a secretarial position in the office of a theatrical agency in order to make the contacts necessary to start her acting career.

A secretarial job can be glamorous; there are many jobs that bring contact with interesting people. To be truthful, though, no matter how glamorous a job is, it cannot be that way all the time. There is the tedious, routine work to be done — completely, accurately, and on time. Correspondence must be completed, reports prepared, files kept — whatever the boss wants done must be done in the way that pleases him.

A *good* secretary is always in demand. Although the exciting parts of the secretarial job are the peripheral duties not attached to the skills, the good secretary will pay attention to the details that are necessary to do an efficient job. When the job market is open, stenographers, typists, and even file clerks are offered secretarial jobs, even though they may lack some of the necessary skills. When the job market is tight, only the totally competent secretary will be found in the better position.

SOCIAL ASPECTS

Working in any office means contact with others. As a secretary, you represent your office, whatever its size, to the public. You will be a public relations person as well as a secretary. To be successful in this endeavor, *look, act, and think success.*

When you want to make an impression on someone, try to look your best. When you enter your office in the morning, look impressive, and you will do a better job and make a better impression on others.

Office Responsibility

As a secretary, you will be in a position to be an office leader because of your relationship with your boss. You will be charged with certain responsibilities. You will set the tone of the office not only in the way your appearance affects others but by the way you act. The way you accept or reject this responsibility will be reflected in the actions of the other employees.

As a secretary, your work may reflect your boss' personality. You will sometimes make minor decisions by assuming the authority to do so – even if you are not completely sure of yourself. If you make mistakes, your boss will probably show disapproval, but a good secretary welcomes constructive criticism with a minimum display of emotion, because of the desire to improve. The good secretary will approach the position as a learning situation. What is learned each day will be reflected in attitude and in work habits.

There will be times when you will find it necessary to fill in for your boss in his absence. You will have to make certain decisions. For those decisions you cannot make, you may find it necessary to postpone action until the boss returns or until additional information can be obtained upon which to base a decision. In either event, good working relationships will be enhanced if you leave the person involved with the feeling that you understand the importance of the problem and that you will have a decision as soon as possible. If necessary, stay in contact frequently enough so that the person will know he has not been forgotten.

For example:

> Assume your boss is on vacation and you have a letter that specifically requests a quick reply. Instead of setting it aside, take action. You might write a letter saying something like, "You indicated in your letter that you need an immediate answer. Mr. Vancil will be out of the office until next week, so I took the liberty of showing your letter to Mr. Arnold. He advised me to tell you that . . ."

A superior secretary uses extreme care to avoid usurping the decision-making powers of his boss. A secretary may have an excellent idea of the direction a decision might take, but will tactfully refrain from making a decision that should be made by an executive.

There are times when a secretary must assume authority. Assumption of authority is something you must accomplish of your own initiative. When the boss is not in the office and it is necessary to reach a decision, act – then explain to the boss what you have done.

You might find it necessary to assume authority to get your boss to take action when it becomes obvious that he is procrastinating on a matter that should be transacted. You may feel the need to prod him into action:

> Assume that you have a file on which a decision must be made, and Mr. Vancil has been putting off making the decision for several days. You can see that a crisis time is approaching. Take action – ask him if he is ready to dictate a response on the file.

Whatever he does, you accomplish your task if you have helped him to accomplish his.

It is certainly true that the secretary is hired because of the value of shorthand and typewriting skills. It is also true that the boss is interested in the total value of the secretary to his office and to the company as a whole. Conversely, it is equally true that an unhappy secretary can be a drawback to both these values. The secretary who is happy on the job will find it much easier to become interested in the work of the office and to understand the policies and procedures of the company.

It is generally recognized that the total secretarial position goes beyond ability in the technical skills; it places the secretary in a position of having to work with people. To be successful as a secretary, it is *vital* that you enjoy your work. You cannot work well with people unless you *like* working with people. It is highly desirable, therefore, to select your job carefully so that you can associate with the type of people you prefer.

If you enjoy social affairs and parties, why not search for a job that will be social in nature? If you find it desirable to work with people who are intellectual, why not choose an educationally oriented place to work — perhaps a publishing company, a book-store, or a school? Nothing is so disastrous to an office as having a misfit in the secretarial position. And nothing is so disastrous to the secretary as *being* a misfit.

If you are happy in your work, you will take pride in doing your job well. You will do the best job of which you are capable, because you will want to keep your job. When you do your job well, the boss will be pleased, and this, in turn, will keep you happy in your work. The happier you both are, the more successful you both will be.

PSYCHOLOGICAL ASPECTS

What kind of person are you? Do you have a quick temper? Do you feel the urge to complain frequently? Do you feel that everyone takes advantage of you? Do you feel you can handle people well? Do you meet people easily? Do people like you? Are you argumentative? Are you shy? Are you bold? Do you laugh readily? Do you cry easily? Do you like to work alone? Do you like to be around others?

Honest answers to these questions will help you to understand yourself better.

Are you frightened of your superiors? Do you panic when they look at you? You will not be happy in your job if you are scared of your boss; but don't confuse fear and respect. You may respect your boss so much that you hesitate to question him, but this is different from being afraid of him.

If your problem is a great respect for your boss (and this can be a problem), then your reactions will be entirely different. You will do the assigned tasks with your usual efficiency, happy when the boss shows approval of your work, but reluctant to assume responsibility to make even minor decisions. This reluctance may make it impossible for you to function as a successful reflection of your boss — to help him as he should be helped — but such reluctance may be overcome as you gain experience.

> One businessman tells of the woman who became a successful secretary in his department and was ultimately offered the opportunity to become a management trainee. When she had finished her management training and was in charge of a unit of the company, he asked her if she could give him some advice in getting his secretary to perform more adequately. Her reply was that the girl was probably scared of him, as she herself had been at one time. He asked her if she was scared of him now, and her reply was, "Not at all." Asked why she had been afraid of him, she said, "I can't tell you why — certainly you have never been difficult to work for, you always took time to explain, and you never lost your temper — but I was afraid of you until I had worked for you for quite a while."

This incident seems to indicate an unsure self-image. It is sometimes difficult for the young secretary on the first job to see a self-image of a mature individual in a mature working world. The young secretary may depend on the boss for explicit instructions on every job function. The mature person will shed this attitude and realize that the boss is not a parent substitute. The mature person will accept adult responsibilities in an office, thus establishing a good rapport with the boss.

If you really *fear* the person for whom you work, perhaps the wisest choice is to find another job; otherwise, you will become a physical and mental wreck. No individual should subject himself to working in a situation where fear is the basic ingredient.

If you are obsessed with an overabundance of respect, bring this into the proper perspective by learning your job well. As you learn your job, continue to respect your boss, but see him for what he is — a human being with personal needs very similar to your own, and with business needs with which you can assist if you do your job properly. When you can see how important you are to him, you will feel more relaxed about your relationship and you will be happier in your work.

I Will Try

Three little words — *I will try* — will help you to be successful in most of your attempts to do what you now think is difficult. It is really amazing what can be achieved when your mind is put to work on personality development.

BEHAVIORAL ASPECTS

What do behavioral standards have to do with secretarial work? There will be times when you will be placed in situations that may be easily misunderstood. The way in which you handle yourself will be important to your professional reputation.

Day-To-Day Situations

The pressure of daily tasks sometimes creates tension that, if not carefully monitored, can result in abrupt answers to questions, and these may appear to others as rudeness. On other occasions, situations may lend themselves to a loss of temper. To illustrate such a situation:

> Jane is working for an executive who is eager to send letters out to a particular group of people, and he tells Jane that another executive's secretary (Maude) will be able to provide the names and addresses. Jane calls Maude and asks if she has the list of names and addresses.

Instead of showing the expected cooperation in producing the list, Maude says that she has the list but she has no time to get it out now, and that Jane will have to wait until the following day.

Stopping at this point, how do you think Jane will react? Will she insist that she must have the list? Will she lose her temper and insist that her work is just as important as Maude's? Will she, out of surprise, agree to wait?

Do you think Maude is deliberately being uncooperative, or do you think she has been told to do nothing until her task at hand has been finished? Are there other reasons her answer might have been given?

How could Maude have avoided creating a situation that might be misunderstood? How can Jane react to retain good human relations and still achieve her goal of obtaining the list?

Jane tells Maude that her boss is very eager to get a mailing out, and she offers to pull the list and make a copy if Maude will take just a moment to tell her where to find it.

Jane has refused to get defensive, angry, or upset. Maude can hardly refuse Jane's request and may even apologize for being so abrupt, indicating that her answers were probably the result of tension and, perhaps, frustration in trying to complete a particular piece of work for her boss. But if Maude continues to give such answers under various circumstances, she may find herself being considered temperamental and difficult to work with. It is up to Maude to decide what her reputation will be, realizing that her reputation is determined by others.

Consider the time when Maude greeted a visitor to the office with, "If you will have a seat you can wait. Mr. Tompkins just called your agent to say that it will be 5 P.M. before he can see anyone — I don't see how you failed to get the message."

What has Maude really said to the visitor? Is she telling him she will *allow* him to wait? Is she implying that something is wrong with the visitor for not having received the message? Is she implying that the visitor got the message but ignored it? Is it any of her business why the message was missed? Does she show concern that the message was not delivered?

The visitor told Maude that he had an appointment for 3:45, that he did not intend to wait until 5:00, and that since he knew Mr. Tompkins was in the office at the moment, he would leave the next move to him. When he left, he was upset because, since there had been several people in the office, he had not taken the opportunity to tell the secretary what he really thought.

What was he really thinking? Do you think he will continue to do business with Mr. Tompkins?

The final result was that a contract involving nearly $40,000 was canceled.

Do you think Maude kept that job after Mr. Tompkins discovered what had happened? No, she lost the position very quickly, for Mr. Tompkins cannot afford to have his clients upset. Maude will need to modify her behavior and learn to monitor her words more carefully. She must listen to herself as others hear her.

Office Parties

Entertainment budgets are sometimes established for various executive levels of business. Christmas parties and banquets have become a part of the business world. A secretary may be invited to attend some of these functions; therefore, behavioral standards become important at this point.

Consider, for example, the situation Sue found herself involved in with one of the young men in her office:

Dan had a very pleasant manner and treated the secretaries very considerately. He talked a lot, boasting to anyone who would listen about all the things he was doing. He promoted the impression of being very important in his field, constantly in demand for his vast knowledge and skill. Dan had asked Sue to do a number of small typing jobs for him, which she did as she could work them into her schedule, although he had access to an office typing pool. One day, he indicated that he wanted to take her to lunch to show his appreciation for her extra efforts to help him. Later, at one of the company dances, he asked her for several dances and filled her ear with pleasant, flattering chatter. The next day, Sue found a single rose on her desk. This was followed by another luncheon, then by dinner and a show.

At the beginning of the following week, Dan asked Sue to do him a very special favor by providing him with information about certain actions her boss was taking concerning the project Dan was working on. She knew that her boss did not think Dan was performing the kind of job that was expected, and that he was considering assigning the project to someone else.

Should Sue have told Dan what she knew? He was asking her to betray one of the basic premises of the secretary's profession — that of loyalty to the boss. Is it ethical for one individual to use another for his own advantage?

If Sue upheld her ethical convictions, she remained loyal to her boss; but she placed herself in the position of being accused of willingness to accept favors such as flowers, dinners, and shows, but unwillingness to reciprocate with favors when asked.

This is the way behavioral standards become important to the secretarial job. If secretaries are aware that such incidents can and do happen, behavior can be determined in advance of a situation, and perhaps the request can be blocked before it is made. Thus the behavioral concept here might best be stated as a question: How friendly can you be with business associates without placing yourself in an awkward situation?

PHYSICAL ASPECTS

The secretarial job may or may not be physically tiring, but it can be emotionally, mentally, and psychologically tiring. Because it is primarily a sedentary job, you should make an effort to get sufficient exercise so that you can be healthy and physically fit.

Physical fitness is important in preventing excessive absences from the office. Although most employers feel that health is more important than the job, they also know that some employees make a concentrated effort to take advantage of every "sick day" they accumulate during a working period, forgetting that sick leave is a benefit — not a right. It soon becomes obvious to a boss when an employee has this attitude. It is a dangerous attitude for two reasons: (1) It places doubt in the mind of the boss about the dependability of the employee; and (2) if the employee *really* got sick — an extended period of time when he needed two or three weeks to recover – the doubt previously raised in the boss's mind would make it difficult for him to retain the employee on the payroll.

Other disadvantages of too many absences are that work accumulates during absences; and that an employee may find that someone else does such an excellent job in his place that his own efforts are shown in a poor light. Try to understand the employer's position. For example;

> Sue accumulated one day per month in sick leave. She made it a practice to take one day off every month by calling in to the office and leaving word that she was not feeling well. One day, Sue had an automobile accident and was hospitalized for a week with a couple of broken ribs. She had no sick leave accumulated, because she had been using it each month.

Can she expect the boss to give her the time she needs? Should she tell him to find someone else? Should she ask him to give her the time she needs without pay?

If she asks him to give her the time she needs, she is asking for an undeserved bonus. The boss will have to pay someone else to do her work while she is away, and he will have to pay her at the same time. Is this a fair approach to the problem?

If she tells him to get someone else, she is placing him in the position of stopping in the middle of whatever he may have scheduled to find a permanent replacement. He will have to go through a training period with this new person without Sue's assistance. Is this fair to him?

If she asks for the time she needs without pay, the boss will have to work with a stranger on a temporary basis – a stranger who will not be particularly interested in the job because it is temporary. Is this fair?

Some people are prone to colds because they won't take care of themselves. Some people are prone to Monday-morning blues or illnesses because of their extensive social weekends. Some people are prone to Friday-afternoon illnesses. These three types of people are unfair to their employers and unfair to themselves.

The employee who has an excellent attendance record for years deserves special consideration when he is ill. When an employee is ill, the boss will want him to stay home and take care of himself, but illnesses that come too frequently are an indication of trouble.

Your physical fitness will make you an asset to the office, and it will be an asset to you. So many opportunities exist in today's world to participate in physical activities that they become social as well as physical, and psychologists tell us that they contribute to emotional and mental health.

VOCATIONAL ASPECTS

Your past training in the secretarial area has consisted primarily of learning skills. You have studied shorthand, and you have probably been taught that you must be able to tell your future employer the speed and accuracy with which you can take dictation. You have studied typewriting, and you have probably taken a tremendous number of speed drills to check the speed and accuracy of your typing. You have studied English or business English so that you can use words properly. You have studied human relations or applied psychology or a related course dealing with human behavior.

What will these isolated subjects do for you on the job? How will you put them to work? Why were they included in your curriculum?

The initial answer to these questions is simply that the employer is interested in your ability to perform in these areas; therefore, they serve to open the door for your entry into the office. When you are filling out the application form, you will find questions relating to the speed of shorthand and typewriting. When you are interviewed, you will be judged by your ability to make a good impression. You may even be given tests that will indicate your ability to work with others.

There is a deeper meaning to these subjects, though, and a greater significance to their inclusion in your curriculum. Your vocational skills will take on a new significance as you put them to work. At times you may feel like a juggler struggling to keep all the balls in the air at the same time, but you must draw your skills and knowledge together in their new role in an office environment.

As you assume the duties of your job, you will find your employer interested in the number of letters you can turn out in a day's work in spite of the fact that you have also answered the telephone, greeted people coming into the office, or run errands. The boss will not sit with a stopwatch in his hand to time your typing speed. He will not dictate by the stopwatch; the speed of his dictation depends upon his ability to organize his thinking. You can expect a variable speed, sometimes more rapid but usually slower than classroom dictation.

Your boss will not expect you to spout rules of grammatical construction or to discuss the formulation of a paragraph, but he will expect you to put this information to use in his correspondence.

The boss will not expect you to develop a psychologist's skill to analyze people in the office or those doing business with the office, but he will expect you to get along with people and to develop a good rapport with them.

The remainder of this book will explore typical situations that you will encounter on the job. Relationships will be examined on an individual and a group basis. Grooming techniques will be covered, to guide you in developing a sense of appropriate dress on the job. Self-control and moderation of emotion will be discussed. Ways of handling awkward and embarrassing situations, how to develop good work habits so that you can enjoy your work, how to understand others better — these are among the topics included in the pages ahead of you.

Take the fundamental concepts developed in this book, add to them several years of experience, and you should find yourself in an interesting and profitable position.

2

The Interview

A secretarial interview provides an opportunity to sell the service that a secretary is able to perform. It is important, therefore, to develop the art of the interview. But how?

Many people tend to think of the interview only in connection with the acquisition of the job. Actually, interview techniques are constantly used in both business and social life. When you meet someone, you interview him to determine if he is the type of person that you want to be friends with, that you want to date, or that you want to avoid. You are interviewed each time someone meets you. The interview, then, is either an informal or a formal conversation in which two people seek to learn more about each other.

You have probably had one or two "blind dates." Didn't you feel just a little more uncomfortable thinking about a date with this unknown person than about one with someone you know? The same is true of a business interview. Because you do not know the person who will interview you, you do not know what to expect; therefore, you feel just a little uncomfortable.

You have met friends of your parents, parents of your friends, and other adults in the community. Stop and think about your reaction to some of these meetings of the past. How did you react? What type of personalities did the people have? Were some easier to meet than others? Were there some that made you uncomfortable? Were there some that caused you to feel comfortable? Were there some that got you tongue-tied? Were there some that made you feel slightly awed?

Which type of person that you have met in the past impressed you the most? Which ones do you remember most vividly? Why?

After Mary took your arm and guided you over to a man and said, "Ann, I want you to meet my father, Mr. Alden; Daddy, this is Ann Phigby," did you initiate the first remarks, or did you wait for Mr. Alden to start the conversation? Were you responsive to his remarks, or did you let the conversation die because you could not contribute? Think of other introductions. Was there a lot of laughter in some instances? Was there a notable lack of humor in some? What kind of person caused you to respond in the most natural manner?

IMPROVING YOUR INTERVIEWING TECHNIQUES

Do you have a friend who seems to be at ease in meeting people — particularly interesting people? If so, why not study the methods used — ask questions such as, "How do you manage to get an introduction, and how do you know the right thing to say?" People are usually flattered to be asked such questions, and in this way you learn techniques used by other people. It is flattering to people to think they have something that someone else desires; and as long as they do not feel threatened in their own relationships, they are usually happy to share their knowledge.

Apply the same conversation tactics to the business world. The people you have been meeting in the adult world are also members of the business world, and they interview people regularly. There will be some difference in the approach because of the differences in motives for the interview, but generally, you can expect the same methods to apply.

PREPARING FOR THE INTERVIEW

Human relations and management courses go into techniques to be used by the interviewer and the interviewee. It is appropriate here to review some of the information and to relate it to the secretarial position. It is a wise person who prepares for a business interview by anticipating the types of information that will interest the interviewer. This is background research that will give you an idea of the information to be exchanged during that particular interview.

Have you thought of calling the receptionist or the present secretary to ask a few questions about the interviewer? Some companies have people who do nothing but interview, and the receptionist might be able to tell you the person most likely to be your interviewer. You have nothing to lose by trying, and you have a great deal to gain if you can obtain additional information.

You have been taught in other courses how to prepare a letter of application, how to prepare a résumé or data sheet, and how to fill out necessary forms before the interview can be conducted. As you go through this preparatory work pay attention to what you say. Perhaps there are areas you will want to expand upon during the interview. For example, you may have had a particular kind of experience (such as the circled item in Figure 2-1) that you feel

PERSONAL DATA SHEET

CLAIRE R. EVANS

June 15, 1972

Address: 2314 S. Lake, Arlington, Florida   Telephone: 904-723-2313

Personal Data: Single female, 5'7", 125 pound redhead

Education:

        Eastwood High School   College Prep.   1966-1970   B Average
        Lincoln, Nebraska

        Florida Junior College Secretarial   1970-1972   B Average
        Jacksonville, Florida

Activities, Honors:

        Worked on high school yearbook staff
        High Honor Roll, Eastwood High School

Special Skills:

        Typewriter--manual, electric, proportionate spaced--50 wpm mailable
        Shorthand--130 wpm general dictation
        Magnetic Card   Adding Machine
        Magnetic Tape   Calculator--rotary and electronic

Experience:

Florida National Bank   Receptionist-   Oct. 1, 1970- $1.85   Part-Time
Arlington, Florida   Typist   Present

First National Bank   Receptionist   June 12, 1970 $1.65   Moved to
Lincoln, Nebraska   Aug. 12, 1970   Florida

Eastwood 5-10 Store   Clerk   June 12, 1969 $1.40   Returned
Lincoln, Nebraska   Aug. 30, 1969   to school

FIGURE 2-1

would be helpful if you were able to explain in more detail than was possible on the application form. The interviewer may refer to something you put on one of the forms, or in your letter (see the note on Figure 2-2). Be prepared to discuss what you have said.

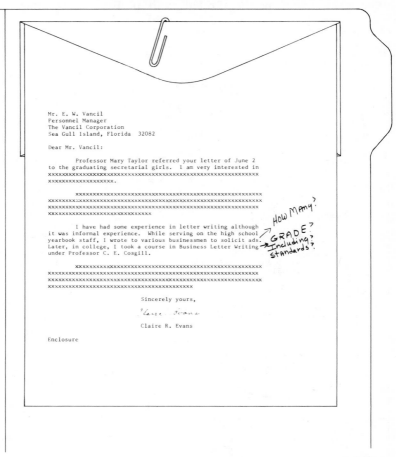

FIGURE 2-2

The application letter and forms constitute your formal portrait to the company. People who take the time to prepare the picture they are presenting frequently find success in obtaining an interview. Typographical errors, errors in format, and careless grammatical errors may not seem particularly important — *but they are*!

When you have a portrait made by a professional photographer, do you allow a strand of hair to be out of place? Or do you want your eyes to sparkle and your face to reflect the best of your physical appearance? Then consider the portrait that you hand to the firm for which you hope to work — any streak, blotch, or blemish should be eliminated from the application form, data sheet, and/or letter, so that the finished product will be attractive.

The Whole-Secretarial Interview

A professional secretary takes an exceptional amount of pride in appearance and in work well done. It is the whole secretary that is of concern to the boss — not the bits of skill and pieces of knowledge you have been developing. Bits and pieces must be developed first, of course, but you are now interested in drawing together your skills and knowledge from your previous courses into a united whole.

Education for the secretary may be compared to the jigsaw puzzle. One piece of the puzzle is set in, then another and another, until the entire picture is complete. Your future employer wants only to look at the whole. The bits and pieces are for reference as needed on the job.

What happens if one piece of a jigsaw puzzle is missing? Isn't there something lacking in Figure 2-3 as you view the whole? What is

FIGURE 2-3

the girl doing? Is she a secretary? Is she a court reporter? Isn't it more satisfying to work a complete puzzle so that you have the

FIGURE 2-4

entire picture, as in Figure 2-4, when you have finished? Now you can tell the entire story — she *is* a court reporter.

The employer wants to know about you. He wants to know your educational record and your work record. Be ready to discuss both. He knows what he is looking for, and he is on a search for all the parts of the puzzle. If one part seems to be missing, he may be disappointed. The only way he can put his puzzle together is by asking questions and getting honest answers from you. You can help him by being prepared for the interview.

You are also seeking to complete the picture puzzle of the firm. There are pieces missing from your picture of it. Will you work primarily for only one person? Will you be assigned to more than one? Is there a central file, or will you keep the records for your office? Are there several secretarial classifications, allowing for promotion? You find answers to these questions during the interview. If you do not find them, you may be disappointed.

As you think about the interview, consider its importance to both participants. The interview has two objectives — first, to give the employer information; and second, to give the applicant information. Therefore, as an applicant, you have a duty and an obligation to both give and receive information. Prepare for an interview — know what you need to share with the interviewer, and know what you wish to find out about the company. With specific objectives in mind, you will have less time to think about being nervous.

When nerves do strike, the best antidote is a few deep breaths to increase your oxygen intake. Pull your breath up from the very tips of your toes — slowly! Exhale very slowly. Repeat this several times and you will feel greatly relaxed. You can also remind yourself that you are the expert on yourself — no one knows more about you than you do; therefore, whatever you are asked you can answer. There may be technical questions with which you might not be familiar. Do not be afraid to say, "I don't know, but I am willing to learn." To some questions, the employer may be hoping for a negative answer, and you will not know which questions these are, so you should be honest and not try to second-guess on the answers. Honesty has a marvelously relaxing effect on nerves.

The Challenge of the Interview

There are jobs, such as the one illustrated in Figure 2-5, that place a great deal of stress and strain on the secretary. If the position

FIGURE 2-5

for which you are being interviewed happens to be of this nature, the interviewer may make an attempt to see how you react under such conditions. This may take the form of making you wait for the interview until you feel like a balloon about to burst, or it may take the form of an abrupt greeting. Will you be ready to accept the challenge of these types of tests? Any situation set up by an interviewer is for the purpose of eliciting information to be used as a basis for selecting the right person for a job.

✓If you were considering spending the rest of your life with someone, how long would it take you to make up your mind that you had found the right person? How hard would you try to get to know him? Suppose you had only twenty or thirty minutes after meeting a stranger to determine if he is the one for you? Could you do it?

This is the position in which the employer finds himself when he interviews you. He will be spending a great many of his waking hours with you — and you with him. It is quite a challenge to decide in such a short time if you two are compatible enough to build a productive office life together.

By studying your application form prior to the interview, the interviewer will have familiarized himself with the type of skills you possess. Depending upon the requirements of his office and upon the amount of information you have already provided, he may have little or no need to question you concerning the skills. There are other duties and responsibilities of the office, and he will have to determine in a very brief period of time whether he feels you will be capable of assuming responsibility. As you study the material in this book, pay particular attention to the various kinds of duties and responsibilities that are described and discussed. In this way, you will become familiar with traits for which an employer may be searching during an interview.

Learning Body Language

As important as words themselves are the actions of the people involved in the interview. Do you realize what you are saying with the muscles of your face, the way you are holding your head, the way you are nodding, the way you hold your hands or motion with them? Body language is becoming an area of study in the field of psychology, and it is very important in the area of business.

An interview is a face-to-face exchange in which much emphasis is placed on body motion as a means of communication. Your posture and body motions tell the interviewer if you are nervous, if you agree with something he is saying, if you disagree, if you are bored or interested. Many things are expressed without uttering one word. Actors at work demonstrate the importance of body actions as they create moods or express feelings without words. Watch your professor — your classmates — your parents — your friends. How much do they say without saying a word? When you know someone extremely well, you can usually judge the mood he is in without hearing him speak.

Practice before your mirror — it really is your best friend. Before a full-length mirror, practice entering the office and greeting your interviewer. Practice seating yourself gracefully in the chair — watch that posture! You musn't appear rigid, but rather, well controlled. Gracefully lean toward him to hand him something and see what effect you create. Talk with him — answer questions you have decided upon in advance. How do your face and body respond as you give your answers? To make this realistic, dress as if you were really there, in order to get the full effect of your actions. Practice to gain poise and confidence.

Study the body actions of others, particularly your professors and friends. It is revealing to park your car in a shopping center during busy hours and watch people going about the business of shopping. You and a friend can analyze whether they are tired or peppy, angry or happy, or even if they are just browsing. Stroll through the stores and notice the communication going on around you. Is that woman tapping her foot because she is impatient at slow service, or angry with her mate, or is she responding to the beat of a musical score?

Watch people walk. How does the "browser" walk? How does the woman hurrying into the store walk? Note the length of stride and the firmness of step. Then watch those two girls dressed in jeans and sandals rushing into the record shop — how does their walk differ from that of the woman?

Watch the students on campus as they study in the library or relax between classes. Can you tell from their posture whether they are interested or bored? Can you tell if they are involved in either study or conversation, or if they are simply wasting time?

As you do these things, you are actually interviewing these people. You are finding out things about them. You may even find an opportunity to enter into conversation with them. For example, while you are standing in line at the grocery store, there is frequent opportunity to interview people and to be interviewed. People who like to talk are easy to interview. People who are bashful are more of a challenge. Speak first; try to open lines of communication. If you meet with rebuff, move on and try again elsewhere. Don't be obnoxious, but practice interviewing whenever you can. You will find your own techniques of asking questions and responding to others getting better every day as you concentrate on improvement; and this in turn will be of inestimable value to you in the formal atmosphere of the business-office interview.

A word of caution – don't be a conversation hog. Once you have made a contribution, let the other person have ample opportunity to talk. Concentrate on keeping the conversation alive and peppy. Keep it interesting to both parties. Take your turn contributing, but don't monopolize.

The Group Interview

The group interview is becoming more and more prevalent in the business world, with two or sometimes more people doing the interviewing as a group, particularly if applicants are expected to work for several people – so maintain your dignity and poise. The group is probably not searching for specific answers, but rather for reactions and attitudes. They want to know, for example, if you have a sense of humor, if you know when to seek assistance, if you know enough to admit you don't know everything. They don't really expect you to be familiar with the policies of the company. They may even try to find out how much agitation you can take and how you will react when you have reached your limit.

A prospective employee should enter into the interview and enjoy it. If you cannot enjoy the interview, you may not enjoy working for the firm, but do not make a snap judgment. Go home and review the interview quietly and in solitude. Analyze what took place in terms of your personal desires. If you enjoyed the interview, why? Was there a particular reason? Was there one person who impressed you? If you did not enjoy the interview, why? Was there an incident that marred the interview for you? Was there a particular person who seemed to bring a negative feeling to you? If so, was there a possible reason for this? Only after you have answered these questions honestly should you make your decision on whether to accept the job should it be offered to you.

Preparing a Portfolio

One of the best ways to prove your interest in the firm and your enthusiasm about getting the job is to carry a portfolio of your work, as artists do.

A portfolio can be as simple as a folder or as elaborate as you wish. The contents should be composed of letters in various styles, reports, memorandums, notices, agendas, and other items you have prepared to give the employer an opportunity to judge the quality of your work. The fact that you have a portfolio with you carries a message that says, "I care." It says you are proud of your work and you want to impress the interviewer. It also says that you put some thought into preparing for the interview.

A professor stressed this idea to a class in Legal Secretarial Procedures, and each student prepared a portfolio.

One of the students later told the professor that she carried the portfolio to an interview with an attorney only because she kept hearing the professor say, "Take it!" She had no intention of using it. She liked the interviewer, the job description, and the beautiful office; but she was getting the brush-off for lack of experience. Figuring that she had nothing to lose, she asked the interviewer to look at samples of her work for Legal Secretarial Procedures. She handed the portfolio to him and crossed her fingers. After studying some of the samples, the interviewer leaned back in his chair and started to ask questions about the class work. A few minutes later, he asked if she could start working immediately.

The fact that something works in one situation does not mean that there is magic in it. Having a portfolio will not assure employment, but it does give you a tiny edge over the applicant who does not have one. Isn't that magic enough to start preparing your portfolio?

Interview Follow-up

Your business portrait is incomplete until a thank-you letter is in the mail. Whether you receive a job offer or not, you should express your appreciation for the time spent with you — the effort expended to give you the opportunity to try for the position. The letter should be fairly brief and not effusive. Let the words be sincere and natural. Be prompt in preparing it, and use the same care as with the application letter.

APPROACHING THE INTERVIEW

Having completed the preparation for an interview, think now about the approach you will use. How can you make a good impression?

Mental Attitude

Approaching an interview with a positive attitude is more likely to bring successful results than approaching it with the idea that you might not get the job. Successful salesmen will affirm that they always approach a sale with the idea that they will succeed.

To achieve the idea of success, review your skills: Where are your strong points? What special skills do you possess? Review your other educational background: Which courses seem to have the most bearing on this particular job? Think about your personality: How will you project your best qualities?

Think about what you will wear to the interview. Coordinate your wardrobe so that you will know you look impressive. Remember as you make your selection to assure comfort as well as style, so that you will be free of any feeling of discomfort, such as from shoes that are too tight.

You have a service to sell — a secretarial service. You know your product can do the job the prospective employer expects. There is every reason to believe your sale will be successful, so approach your interview with confidence.

A Practice Interview

Imagine yourself in an office waiting for an interview. You have been waiting for about twenty minutes when a secretary speaks your name:

"Miss Phigby, Mr. Vancil will see you now." She shows you into the office and Mr. Vancil rises to greet you. The secretary introduces you: "Mr. Vancil, Ann Phigby."

What response would you make? Would you be aggressive and offer to shake hands? Would you greet Mr. Vancil and sit down in the nearest chair? Would you greet Mr. Vancil and wait for him to indicate whether he wishes to shake hands and to offer you a chair?

The interviewer should have the prerogative of guiding the interview; therefore, wait for him to indicate whether he wishes to shake hands or to offer you a chair. When he does invite you to sit, he may indicate, by word or gesture, where he prefers you to sit.

Suppose he then says:

"Your name intrigues me — what is the national origin of it?"

What will your answer be?

He may then say:

"I notice you have recently moved into this area — have you had any difficulty getting settled?"

How would you answer? Would you go into detail about the situation or would you answer briefly and indicate that you are happy with your arrangements?

The questions above are one way an interviewer may use to set a friendly tone for the interview and to give you a chance to overcome any nervousness you may feel. Therefore, all your answers to such questions should be friendly but brief.

Mr. Vancil might advance the interview by asking:

"How did you find out about this opening — did you read our ad or were you referred to us by someone?"

Such a question gives you the opportunity to explain why you applied. For example, you might say that the ad had particularly appealed to you because it was so different from the other ads. It was larger and it read as though the job was important to the company. Or you might say that one of your friends had heard of the job and had suggested that you apply. Whatever the answer, it should in some way indicate that you are interested in learning more about the job.

Mr. Vancil might then ask you a question such as:

"I see that you hold an associate degree in secretarial science from the community college. What, exactly, *is* an associate degree in secretarial science?"

Now you are getting into the depth of the interview — you have the opportunity to explain the unique features of your own secretarial-training background that will be of advantage on the job, such as the study of the proportionally spaced typewriter or the magnetic-tape selectric typewriter, or the course in duplicating techniques. You might explain about the courses that you took other than skills courses — such as Human Relations, Introduction to Data Processing, or Introduction to Business. Here, of course, you would select those courses in your curriculum that most nearly fit into this particular company's work. If you are applying to a clothing firm, for example, you could mention the course in merchandising management that you took during the fall quarter last year.

Now, suppose Mr. Vancil asks you:

"Do you think you will be happy as a secretary?"

Would you rush to assure him that you would be happy to be a secretary the rest of your life? Would you indicate that you know you can be a good secretary after you learn to function with him and that, at this time, you are less sure of what the future might hold? Which answer would you select? Why?

An honest answer is always best. To try to determine the type of answer the employer wants is often a mistake. "To thine own self be true" is a very good quote to remember when you are faced with a question with two or more possible answers.

Then, suppose Mr. Vancil asks you:

"Would you have any objection to working late occasionally if the need arises?"

What would your answer be? "None at all"? "No, but I would like to have an hour or so's notice in order to change any other plans I might have made"? "I really don't like to work late, but if it is necessary to get a job finished, I would be at my desk to help"? "My husband objects to my working late and insists that I be at home in the evening"? Again, an honest answer puts you on an honest basis with the interviewer.

It is only fair to each participant that each provide honest responses during an interview. There are two very important decisions being made, and each is dependent on the honesty of the interview.

As you study the remainder of this book, continue to practice the art of interviewing. By the end of this course, your practice should have prepared you to be ready for success in your real job interview.

Suggested Projects

To discover "How Tense Are You?" arrange to play "The Game-Game Show," a panel show for which the professor has complete instructions.

Arrange for three or four professors or administrators to come to the classroom to interview the students for the position of secretary. When all interviews have been completed, ask the interviewers to give their impressions of their success. Ask questions that may have occurred to you during your own interview.

Arrange for a member of the State Employment Agency or a personnel manager of a local business firm to visit the classroom and talk with you about the interviewing techniques used by that agency or firm in screening applicants for various jobs, particularly secretarial positions.

3

Develop
A Style
of Office Dress

Developing a style of office dress requires attention to many facets of fashion, personality, and acceptability. A fashion can be described as the style accepted and used by most people of taste at a given time. In an office situation, we are concerned not only with fashion but also with appropriateness. The ability to recognize what is both attractive and appropriate is referred to as taste. Clothing that is appropriate for beach wear is not appropriate for the office. Clothing appropriate for a party may or may not be appropriate for the office, depending upon the type of office. Acceptance of a fashion need not be universal; therefore, a style may be adopted in one office or company but would be in poor taste in another.

SOCIAL CONFORMITY

Normal behavior patterns and standards for body cover are generally considered to be rooted in the values of the older generation. Young people, when striving to find their own identity, like to dress in a style they feel is avant-garde or different, thus establishing their role in society. They are seeking recognition — a very normal reaction, indulged in by every generation. As maturity is reached, self-confidence and self-esteem are established, and young people, now mature, find it possible to conform to some of the values of the older generation. Each generation brings some modification into the existing values; and it is through these changes that the business world recognizes changing patterns of dress. The jumpsuit in the illustration on the preceding page is inappropriate and unacceptable. Why? Because the other office workers reject it. If the other workers approved it, the decision on acceptance would then move to the management level. Social conformity, then, seems to be identified as the pattern of dress or behavior that is admired and respected in the particular period of time for a particular purpose.

First impressions assume importance because people are frequently judged by them. A false first impression may endure, even though there is opportunity to become more familiar with the individual.

First impressions are based in large part on the manner of behavior and the style of dress. The style that is acceptable for the classroom is not necessarily the accepted style for the office environment. There is no monopoly on a mode of dress for any generation. Current hairstyles and modes of dress can also be found in old issues of fashion magazines, or even in family picture albums. The short, swingy skirts of the 1920's became the miniskirts of the 1970's. The midiskirts of the 1970's were "reruns" of the skirts worn in the late 1940's. The hairstyles of today's women are reminiscent of times gone by, and the styles adopted by men of the 1970's can be found in pictures of men in the early part of the century.

Are the social styles, however, the styles that will be accepted in the business world? Think about the gum-chewing, purse-swinging, short-skirted, painted doll who applied for the receptionist's position. Did she make the impression necessary to get the job? Think about the long-haired, bearded, sockless giant, who overwhelmed the office staff with his individualized male image, who applied for the management-trainee program. Was he accepted?

THE ACCEPTABLE LOOK

Employers are usually not interested in highly individualized styles, because they do not create the impression of the responsibility, stability, and dependability needed to get a job done efficiently and effectively. Businessmen are interested in the person who can make a successful first impression on a customer. Employers are profit-minded and associate success with community acceptance. Therefore, while some modification in appearance can be accepted, excessive deviation from the current standard is generally not acceptable in the business world.

Achieving the Look of Success

The look of success almost defies description. It is not possible to tell you what you should wear, how you should do your hair, or how much perfume or aftershave lotion to use. Anyone can tell you, however, when the combination is wrong. Achieve the look of success by studying your community. Analyze the wearing apparel and the physical appearance of people engaged in office work, as well as the overall appearance of the offices in your community. In this way, judge what is acceptable there and what seems to be in poor taste. If you plan to work in an insurance office, visit insurance offices and observe the way the secretaries dress. Talk with people employed in offices in your community about acceptable looks, to form a base against which to judge your own look of success.

Personal habits play a part in the look of success. Is gum chewing acceptable in the type of job you hope to obtain? Is smoking acceptable? Do employees snack or eat lunch at their desks? Do they drink coffee at their desks? To what extent are these personal habits practiced? Is there a difference in custom between small offices and large offices?

Responsibility for Dress

The only person who can take the responsibility of achieving the look of success for you is *you*. Only you can do the background research to determine the acceptable standard for looks in your community. This is the type of responsibility that an employer admires in a prospective employee. The transition from student to employee is no easier than the transition between childhood and adulthood; but it is a transition that can be made easier through your research efforts. If you are reluctant to take the responsibility of conducting such research, you may also be reluctant to accept responsibility that may bring you closer to success on the job.

Judging Proper Attire

Research can be exciting when one becomes personally involved. Personal involvement requires identification of a goal to be achieved through research. One such goal might involve a compromise between the social styles of your generation and the styles accepted in the business offices of your community. Another goal might be to determine how much of your current wardrobe can be used in the business world and what needs to be added to it to achieve the successful look.

Changing Looks

Looks change according to the needs and demands of the public. As soon as a fashion is accepted, it begins to look ordinary. Fashion leaders seek something new in fashion, which is then gradually adopted by the majority. With the help of television, newspapers, and magazines, fashion news spreads more rapidly today than ever before, and thus changes are brought about faster.

Styles acceptable for office wear have been changing rapidly, but not at the pace of social fashion. The difference in pace has sometimes created a problem in finding on the racks of department stores suitable clothing for the office. This is particularly true in women's clothing — to the extent that the art of sewing is important to the development of many wardrobes for the office.

Color, always a major consideration in women's clothing, has become popular in most fashions for the business office. The technology of the fashion industry in developing colors that do not fade or change, and fabrics that are easily cleaned, has contributed greatly to the acceptance of color for business clothing.

Textures developed in newer materials used for clothing have made possible a wider selection of clothes acceptable as office attire. Texture is also considered in determining the appropriateness of an article of clothing for the office. The style of a satin dress may be beautiful, the color rich and magnificent, but its texture makes it unacceptable in the business office. It may someday become acceptable, but until that time, it should be reserved for social wear. A heavy wool suit may be quite appropriate for the office in New York City, but the texture might render it unacceptable for the office in Miami Beach. A bathing suit might be appropriate in the office of a water-skiing rental agency, but both the texture and the style would render it unacceptable in other offices of the same community.

Short-lived fashions, lasting only a season or so, are referred to as *fads*. Young people are particularly susceptible to fads. Styles that remain in good taste over a period of time are referred to as *classics*. The conservative business world is inclined toward the classic more than toward the fad as a standard of dress, but there will be an overlap of both seen in the modern office.

The extent of change in business offices must be judged on the community level. As you move from one community to another, you will note that acceptable attire in office wear changes to some degree.

BEHAVIORAL CONCEPTS

Once the look of success has been achieved, the potential employee may begin to explore facets of the business world that will lead to success on the job. As personal habits are an integral part of the overall appearance of the office, so behavioral patterns reflect personal attitudes toward policies of the business office.

Reciprocal Behavior

One of the basic behavioral concepts governing the actions of employees is loyalty to the employer. Having agreed to work, the employee is obligated to concern himself with at least the minimum expectations of the employer. This concept is sometimes referred to as the *principle of reciprocal behavior*, and sometimes as the *Golden Rule* – "Do unto others as you would have them do unto you." The name of the concept is unimportant, but the principle is important to the efficiency and effectiveness of the business organization. Every person is concerned primarily with himself. His likes, interests, and aspirations must be considered by others. Here, "every person" includes the employer.

The dictionary meaning of *secretary* is insufficient. The word originated from the words "secret writer." Therefore secretarial responsibility includes the handling of material and information in a way that protects its confidentiality. A superior secretary feels a primary loyalty to the immediate supervisor, and an overall loyalty to the firm. Only in this way is it possible to attain the degree of confidence necessary to promote a good working relationship between the secretary and the boss.

A second behavioral concept involves the social and psychological needs of oneself and others (remember the discussion in Chapter 1?). The style of dress and individual manner of employees may frustrate, shock, or please the employer, thus fulfilling or denying his need for respect, recognition, or status. The ability to judge the effect is based on a feeling for communications and human relations. If one person compliments another, he is placing a sanction of approval on appearance or action. If compliments are never voiced, something must be wrong. The same elements of judgment are present whether with your employer or with people working near you. Why be so concerned about the approval of other people in office? The answer to this question is rooted in the reciprocal-behavior concept: You seek their approval, consciously or unconsciously, as they seek yours. The person who maintains a selfish attitude and reflects a lack of concern for fellow workers seldom finds himself able to work effectively with other members of the office staff.

LOOKS AND PROMOTIONS

There are times when jobs or promotions depend on a hairstyle, the wise use of cosmetics, or the correct combination of clothes. To be successful, it is necessary to acquire the concepts of good taste in office dress.

Here is what happened when one businessman interviewed a young man for a position:

> The young man wore bell-bottom pants with a pullover shirt, and loafers with no socks. His hair was hanging just below his ears, and he sported a small but neat beard. This mode of dress was acceptable student attire, fashionable on the college campus. The businessman told the young man that although he met the major qualifications for the job, he was not going to be hired. The employer then drew a comparison between the young man's appearance and the appearance of men at work in the large office. The young man listened, then thanked the employer for his honest concern. He said that for the first time someone had told him how he should dress for an interview.

He made a very good impression on the interviewer by saying that he would be ready for the next interview.

> In this same office, two young women were being considered for a promotion. The loser was told that her long hair, streaming across her shoulders, had caused her to lose the chance to advance. She immediately restyled her hair and informed her supervisor that she would be ready for the next promotional opportunity.

Her excellent attitude greatly impressed her supervisor. He realized that had he failed to be honest with her, he might have been the cause of her next failure.

The two young people described above have mastered the art of taking constructive criticism and making it work to their advantage. Most young people are willing to learn — and the best way to learn is to watch, listen, read, ask questions, and think. The sincere employee will recognize that his successful look may have an effect on his advancement opportunities.

SHOPPING TECHNIQUES

Many business people maintain two wardrobes — one for the office and one for social life. Unable to find appropriate business clothes on the clothing racks of the stores, one young woman supervisor circumvented the fashion designers by turning to her trusty sewing machine to construct her office wardrobe. Sometimes it is necessary to learn a new skill, such as sewing, in order to achieve a bigger goal in life.

Comparison Shopping

Whether you select clothes from the rack or create your own wardrobe, the best selections are made only by researching all available merchandise. Compare quality and style, consider durability and upkeep, and concern yourself with color of fabric as it relates to your individual complexion.

Many secretaries make an art of shopping. They learn where they can find appropriate clothes, then cultivate the acquaintance of a salesperson. When you are recognized as a regular customer, you can often determine when clothing will be put on sale and what the price reduction will be. By buying during sales, you can save quite a bit of money on each article. The same approach can be taken toward the purchase of materials.

Comparison shopping involves studying styles and the appropriateness of the style for office wear. Clothes should also fit the personality of the individual and blend with the complexion. Clothes should also be chosen with the physical actions of the job in mind. If much stooping and bending is required on the job, the clothing will need to be of a style that will lend itself to those physical exertions if you are to be comfortable as you work.

Color Coordination

The selection of clothes will include emphasis on style, fabric, and color that are suitable to the individual figure, the climate, the complexion, and the job. The color and fabric chosen will sometimes require a change in the shade of cosmetics used in order to obtain the desired overall look of success. Some color combinations will be flattering to a particular complexion. The skin tone changes in individuals, however, with a change in the color of clothes worn. Usually such skin-tone changes can be altered through the use of cosmetics to permit the wearing of various color combinations, even though they may not be as flattering as others.

Some color combinations are more flattering to the figure of an individual that are others. Although a dress or suit looks most attractive on the rack, the best guarantee of suitability is to try it on in front of a three-way mirror. Some color combinations and styles seem to add weight; others seem to subtract weight. Compare the people in Figure 3-1; which of them needs to focus more attention on selection practices?

The woman on the right is obviously buying clothes that are too young in style, and too small in size. What makes the dress appear young? Take away the horizontal stripes, and the dress becomes a plain style that would be suitable for any age. Horizontal stripes also add the appearance of weight to a figure, whereas a plain line is slimming. The length of the dress can also have a slimming effect, and if this woman had selected a skirt that was several inches longer, she would be more attractive.

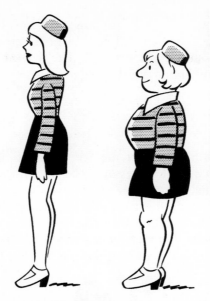

Clothes should fit the age and figure

FIGURE 3-1

Selection Practices

· *Buy in haste, repent at leisure* might be a guiding principle in selecting clothes. Good selection practices require time for making decisions based on color coordination, quality and style, durability and upkeep, and suitability for the job. A woman will consider makeup colors, her figure, and the amount of stooping, walking, and bending that she will be doing. A man will consider his complexion, color of shirt and tie to be worn, and how well the material will hold a crease or resist soil. The woman will consider the purse and shoes to be used with the garment. The man will consider the color of socks and shoes to be worn. The time devoted to clothes selection may involve days, sometimes weeks, of thought.

Pattern and fabric selection, when you make your own clothes, will involve the same decision-making process. One major difference will involve the inability to try on the product — relying instead upon trying to visualize the finished effect. An advantage in this area is that more expensive materials may be used, allowing the wardrobe to take on a richer tone of quality, provided time is allowed and sufficient skill utilized in the construction of the garment.

Care in the selection process will result in creating the impression of a "fashion plate," which means that you are appropriately and stylishly dressed. The bonus comes when your looks enhance your opportunities for success.

VISUAL IMPRESSIONS

Everyone dresses to create an impression. The impression actually made may not necessarily be the impression the person hopes he is making. Before wearing a new dress or suit to the office, stand before a full-length mirror and go through every motion apt to be made in the daily office routine. Bend over the boss's desk to point out some item, and view your derriere in the full-length mirror; remember that this is the view others see of you. Look at Figure 3-2.

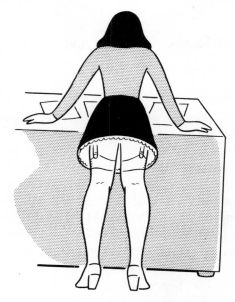

FIGURE 3-2

This can happen so easily. Unless the secretary practices movements in front of a mirror, she may be unaware that it happens to her. Figures 3-3 and 3-4 show a more acceptable appearance for this activity. Stoop to the level of the lowest drawer of the filing cabinet, and view yourself in the full-length mirror. Sit down and prop your

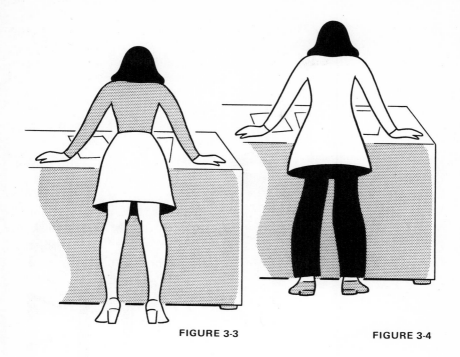

FIGURE 3-3   **FIGURE 3-4**

feet up, or cross your legs — do you present an attractive picture? Study Figure 3-5. The posture is good, but what detracts from the appearance of this young lady? There is only one solution — lowering the hemline, as shown in Figure 3-6.

Charm experts tell us that clothing provides an opportunity to express personality. The way you dress conveys your philosophy of life and your taste and feel for aesthetics, as well as reflecting your personal habits. Does your mirror image reflect the personality you feel is you?

Analyze the Job

Of course, you see all sorts of clothing in some of the modern offices. Analyze the kinds of jobs done and how active each person must be in his job; then ask yourself if the dress is appropriate. What kind of impression will be made? Be governed by good taste and logic, as well as style.

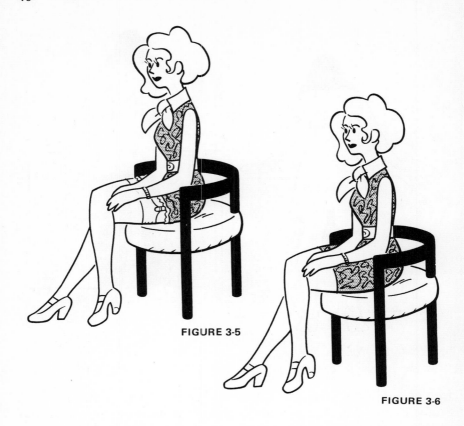

FIGURE 3-5

FIGURE 3-6

Analyze Your Figure and Age

The type of clothing that is worn is less important in conveying the image than what is done with the solid material that fills the clothing. Compare how the miniskirt, the maxiskirt, and the midiskirt will look on the small-boned, fragile type of girl; the tall, gangly, thin girl; the raw-boned, pioneer type of girl; and the stocky, heavy girl. Compare a man in sport shirt, jeans, and sandals to one in suit, shirt, and tie, with polished shoes and dark socks. Who looks more mature — and wise? Fashion designers always say that the chic individual is one who is dressed in a manner appropriate for weight, height, color, and age. For business, we might add to these criteria the approriateness for the job.

Analyze Trends

Fashion trends — mini, maxi, or whatever — are trends that may or may not be appropriate for a job. Remember that if you crave the

latest fashion, there is always your free time in which to experiment. The time may come when hostess pajamas will be worn to the office — or futuristic jump suits — but for now, don't be too eager to wear the latest fashion on the job.

APPROPRIATE HAIRSTYLES

Since hairstyles contribute to overall appearance, they, like clothing, express your personality. Some women look cute, some look sophisticated, some are beautiful, and some look wholesome. Men look neat, sloppy, shaggy, fatherly, or trustworthy. What look describes you?

Analyze Bone Structure

Your hairstyle should be governed to the greatest extent by the bone structure of your face and the stature of your body. One way for a woman to determine her best style is to visit a wig shop or beauty salon and spend time trying on various styles of wigs. Try on short ones, long ones, curly ones, straight ones, dark ones, and light ones. Note what each does in relationship to your bone structure, your skin tone, and the color of your eyes. Find out which styles suit you best. Ask the saleslady to help you in this area. Try on wiglets to augment your own hairstyle; try braids, buns, curl clusters.

Large department stores and wig shops train their salespeople, usually quite extensively. Large wig manufacturers supply training sessions for sales personnel, geared to successful fitting and styling to suit individual needs of the clientele. In smaller stores or discount houses, such expert help may not be available. To receive expert assistance, consult a specialist in the area of hairstyles and wigs — whether a beauty-salon stylist or the trained personnel of the major department stores or wig shops.

Wigs and wiglets are a good investment for use at times when your own hair isn't up to par for the day; but nothing substitutes for your own gloriously clean, well-groomed hair. A wig or wiglet kept in the office desk can give you that particular lift you need when an unexpected important occasion arises in the office, or when that hoped-for, but unexpected, big date comes along.

Analyze Hair Color

Many secretaries use hair-coloring techniques to individualize their appearance, to cover prematurely gray hair, or to change their image altogether by completely altering the color of their hair. The natural color should not be changed on a whim — there should be a very good reason. If you feel you *must* do something to change your hair color, remember that the process is much easier by using a wig than by dyeing your own hair. You may find that the color you want does not look natural — particularly if you are changing dark hair to light hair. If you are really serious, try a different shade of cosmetics, and you might be able to alter your skin tone to be compatible with the hair color, so that it will appear natural. If you are absolutely sure that you now want to change your own hair color, you know how it will look and the exact shade you are striving to achieve.

Analyze Hair Growth

Give thought to the speed with which your hair grows. Once you begin to change color, be prepared to keep a regular schedule of treatments; since appearance is so important in the office, you should never be caught with that natural shade showing.

Hair growth is also important in maintaining the style in which the hair is worn. A regular trim or cut can be most important to your appearance. Determine how often a cut is needed, and arrange your schedule to include regular care.

Analyze Hair Problems

If you discover certain problems with your own hair, such as dandruff, limpness, or dullness, consult your druggist or beautician for tips on shampoo or conditioning agents to be used for your hair health.

Suitable for Work . . . Suitable for Play
FIGURE 3-7

Style your hair in a simple set for the office, saving the elaborate hairstyle for dates or parties. Not only will you be more appropriately dressed for the office, you will feel very special when you have that date or attend that party, because you actually alter your personality impression to some degree when you change your hairstyle or hair color.

FIGURE 3-8

Figure 3-7 shows an acceptable office hairstyle and an elaborate hairstyle. Figures 3-8, 3-9, 3-10, and 3-11 illustrate acceptable hairstyles for the business office. Note particularly the facial bone structure and the way the hair style emphasizes the best features.

APPROPRIATE COSMETICS FOR WOMEN

Women use cosmetics to enhance their beauty; clowns use them to create faces that cause laughter. Unfortunately, some women

FIGURE 3-9

unintentionally use them the same way. In the business office, cosmetics should be used moderately, to accentuate natural beauty but not to attract undue attention.

Which of the eyes in Figure 3-12 accentuates natural beauty?

Experimentation is again the best way to determine the most flattering shade and appropriate amount of makeup. Here again, the advice of the saleslady at the cosmetics counter may be helpful. Usually these women have been trained to match various cosmetics with skin tones. Some lines of cosmetics have been especially developed for young people; some are developed primarily for other age groups.

Selection Techniques

Some cosmetics are developed to apply to very dark skin, some to eliminate color casts that are due to illness or chemical change in skin tone. You must determine the shades meant for you. When you

FIGURE 3-10

FIGURE 3-11

52

Suitable for Work . . .   **. . . Suitable for Play**

FIGURE 3-12

do not feel well, your skin tone changes and you may need different shades of makeup from those you normally use. What you need is determined by your skin tone and texture. Your analysis of your cosmetic needs will assure a nice appearance even when you can't look like your usual cheery self.

One good basic rule is to select one line of cosmetics that complements your skin tone and purchase a basic set of makeup in that line. This basic set may contain eye makeup, or you may wish to purchase eye makeup in a different line. Mixing cosmetics freely, however, can have less-than-attractive results because of the interaction of the ingredients used in the various lines.

Proper selection of cosmetics makes it possible to cover skin blemishes, and even scar tissue. Your druggist can be helpful in the selection of cosmetics for these purposes.

Makeup becomes stale and rancid after about five months. Using old makeup may create complexion problems such as clogged pores. Cake powder, moisturizers, astringents, perfume, and cologne become rancid, so keep your supply fresh.

Some people's skin needs less makeup than does others'. Does your skin repel or absorb makeup? There is no need to buy makeup you cannot use. Your experimentation should help you determine what you do need, and the shade that is most complimentary.

The Natural Look

Strive for the natural look as you experiment with applying your makeup. When you add a new product to your beauty regimen, practice until you can apply is so skillfully that it looks natural. The basic ingredient to a natural look is a clean, radiant skin. Too much makeup not only hides the radiance of your skin but can contribute to skin problems. If you have a skin problem, your druggist may recommend a special soap that will help clear it up. If it persists, consult a dermatologist.

Basic Skin Care

Whatever your skin type, the moisture in night cream will be absorbed within five or ten minutes of its application; therefore, there is no need to go to bed a greasy mess. Removing the excess cream also allows your skin to breathe at night, to retain its healthy glow.

Dust your dresser before you go to bed tonight, and in the morning run your finger across its surface. You will note a slight dust film, even in an air-conditioned room. Remember that this same film of dust has settled on your face during the night, and it should be removed before makeup is applied for the day.

The Natural Eye Look

Eye makeup is selected to blend with your makeup and with the colors of your clothing. Applying the color to look natural and enhance the color and shape of your eyes requires practice and patience.

False eyelashes should not be used in a business office unless you have a special problem. If they are worn during office hours, trim them carefully to present a natural look.

The Finished Look

An unfinished look results when makeup stops at the chin line. Think about makeup for your neck area. The color of the neck may be entirely different from that of the face and may require a different shade of makeup, which should then be blended in the chin–lip area. The extension of makeup to the neckline of your clothing creates the finished look you must have.

Emergency Repairs

What do you do if you are caught in the rain during your lunch hour? Have you thought of keeping a makeup kit and a set of electric curlers in your desk? These shouldn't be used on office time, of course, but you could use part of your lunch hour or coffee break to repair any damage you may have sustained.

APPROPRIATE GROOMING FOR MEN

The modern man is concerned with more extensive grooming practices than were men in past generations. With the upsurge in the use of lotions, colognes, and hair-grooming products, and the changing trend of dress, there is a need to discuss grooming techniques.

The Clean-Face Look

If you are seeking employment in a regular business office, you may find more success without facial hair. An interviewer is seeking an attractive, intelligent, personable young man as judged by his own standards of these qualities; and while it is true that you see some beards and mustaches on faces in the offices, these may have been acquired after employment. Grooming techniques do reflect an individual's personality, his value judgments, and his personal habits; therefore, he will be judged by the impression he makes in an interview.

Beards are, of course, of varying quality — some easy to control, some more difficult. The man with a fast-growing beard may find it necessary to shave several times a day to maintain the look of integrity so important when handling customers. For this reason, some businessmen keep an electric razor in a desk drawer to use just prior to an appointment or a meeting.

Shaving lotions are marketed today in a wide variety of scents. A lavish application can result in an unpleasant aroma, but a sparing application adds much to the attractiveness of the male image. Shaving lotion, like perfume, should be used to enhance the personality of the individual — not to kill all the mosquitos in the room.

The Bearded Look

All hair — head or facial — should be kept clean and well groomed. Men style their hair just as women do, and the style should fit the physical build, the facial contours, and the personality. Strike

FIGURE 3-13

a happy balance. Some young men try the bearded look; for some it is an improvement, and for others pure disaster.

If your appearance does represent the real you, then would it be dishonest to represent yourself as a clean-faced personality when you really prefer the bearded look? The question to be resolved is whether the real you *is* represented by the bearded look and whether you feel you can be effective without it, knowing that greater success might come with fairly short hair and without either beard or mustache. If either is retained, a trim, neat look will cause it to be more acceptable than a wild, bushy look. Figure 3-13 shows two views of the same man. The business world would probably prefer the clean-shaven look, but might accept the neatly trimmed mustache and beard if the position has infrequent contact with customers or clients, or if the business is one in which facial hair is common. You can judge whether your style will be successful by observing men holding positions similar to the one for which you will be applying.

HAND CARE

Hands are constantly on display in the office. Long fingernails are impractical when you use the typewriter, so determine a reasonable length for both looks and efficiency. If you have difficulty growing nails or have weak nails, gelatin capsules (available in the supermarket) are said to add strength. An application of white iodine to the tips of your fingers will heal small abrasions and discourage the biting of nails.

Chipped nail polish detracts from an otherwise pleasing appearance; so, for the office, a natural or very light shade of polish will be most effective. Buffing nails brings out the natural shine attractive on the hands of both men and women. The use of whitener under the nails will help to avoid the grinding of carbon and other discolorants into them.

THE TOTAL LOOK

Psychologists tell us that we do our best work and our best thinking when we look our best; therefore, the psychological qualities of beauty are important to you. *Think pretty*, and you will be pretty. *Think manly*, and you will be manly. Coordinate your clothes, your hairstyle, and your makeup, and you will be at your best.

The "hippies" of the 1960's, the "swingers" of the 1950's, the "jitterbuggers" of the 1940's and the "flappers" and "sheiks" of the 1920's — not one of these groups represents the business world of its generation, because the business world seeks the average in behavior and dress. The term "average" is, of course, difficult to define and changeable in character. Average behavior and dress can be best described as what is acceptable under given circumstances and at given times. Be flexible and willing to change, but first take time to analyze what the change will do for you in the office environment. Only when you have determined that the change will be appropriate should you make it.

Suggested Projects

Invite a local cosmetician, beautician, or fashion designer to lecture on his or her specialty, with emphasis on the business look. Set up a discussion period during which the students can ask individual questions.

Before issuing the invitation, hold a class discussion to determine possible guest lecturers, so that you can select the best one available. Select several alternate dates, so the lecturer will have a choice of the best time for his schedule.

To obtain the best results, explain the nature of your study regarding office dress, and provide a few specific ideas of what you expect to learn from him.

Invite a local businessman or businesswoman to lecture on "Office Dress." Follow the recommendations in the first suggestion in selecting the lecturer.

Arrange a panel discussion on "Office Dress." The panel might consist of students, secretaries, businessmen, or a combination thereof.

Arrange a style show to demonstrate clothing, hairstyles, and makeup appropriate to the business world and to the social world. Perhaps you can gain the cooperation of local businesses in this venture. If the approach is right and the explanation is clear, businessmen will usually respond to such requests. If possible, schedule the style show in an auditorium or other large-group meeting place, and invite all students and faculty to attend. Models can be obtained from your class or from other student groups in the college. Introduce some wild styles to add humor, interest, and contrast to the show.

You are a secretary in a large department store. Your boss is in charge of arranging fashion shows for both men and women, to interest them in spending their money in order to be well dressed.

Each time your boss arranges a showing, he does research to match hairstyle, cosmetics, and accessories with the costumes. Sketches 1, 2, and 3 (to be supplied by the professor) show three costumes. Your boss wants you to look through style books, newspapers, old magazines, and so on, to bring together several hairstyles appropriate to each costume, so that he can make a choice for the showing. If you are unable to clip the picture of the hairstyle, sketch it in pencil and attach it to the costume sketch.

Your boss has been asked to speak to a Secretarial Procedures class at the local community college on appropriate business dress for the office. He has asked you to help him with research for this speech. He wants you to go to various business offices and observe the following (make notes so that you can give him accurate information):

A. *Number of offices you observe*
B. *Approximate length of skirts*

C. *Kinds of necklines of female employees*
D. *1-2-3 order of preference of female employees for suits, blouses and skirts, dresses*
E. *1-2-3 order of preference of male employees for suits, white shirts, non-white shirts, ties, and sport shirts*
F. *What kind of ties are preferred, color and style*
G. *Height of heels on women's shoes*

Your boss has given you 48 hours to make your survey and get your findings to him. (Remember, you still have your other duties to take care of as well — you must work this into your schedule as you can.)

4

Develop
An Office
Personality

One of the most important aspects of office efficiency is the ability of each employee to work effectively with all others. Many psychological tests have been developed, and are currently in use in the business world, to test just such compatible working attitudes and personality traits.

SELECTION OF AN OFFICE STAFF

An office staff is handpicked to function as a team. Each office worker is selected for personal traits and qualities, as well as for professional skills. If the administrator making the decision on the hiring of a person does not think he will fit into the social atmosphere established by others in the office, the applicant will not be hired regardless of the skills he possesses. What is the reason? Because people must be able to work together if they are to do the most efficient job—and one person causing disruptions can make an office efficiency rating plummet downward.

As a secretary, you will be a very important part of the office staff—an important member of the office team. Your position provides the liaison function between your boss and the office staff. You will be responsible for developing and maintaining a smooth flow of communications between yourself and others in the office in order to fulfill this liaison function.

JOINING THE TEAM

When you first walk into an office to take on the duties and responsibilities of a new job, you will probably feel very alone. You are new, and you are a stranger. To fit in, you must look and act confident even if you feel otherwise. It will take time for you to develop into a functioning member of the office team.

The first step in joining the team is to develop rapport with the members already on the team. Observe things you have in common with other members of the office staff. These commonalities will provide opening remarks in conversation. Everyone seeks to fulfill his own needs before meeting the needs of others; therefore, if you place emphasis on others, you will find them responsive to you. They will be drawn to you because you make them feel important. As you develop friendly relations with other staff members, you will be creating solid relationships that can be used in fulfilling organizational objectives. Through your discussions, you will come to understand the purposes of the organization and the way these purposes are to be fulfilled. You will find yourself supporting the purposes of the office, building loyalty to the organization, becoming part of the office team. You will find yourself working with others to fulfill the goals of the organization.

PERSONALITY TRAITS

You may find it necessary to alter your personality somewhat to allow you to function more efficiently as a team member. You may, for example, have to learn to control your temper instead of issuing a stinging comment when you are displeased. You will need such control when minor irritations arise, so that you present a picture of a calm person totally in command of the situation.

Suppose, for example, that you have need for a particular set of addresses, and you are instructed to obtain them from another secretary. You call her on the phone and ask if she has the list. Her response is as shown in Figure 4-1. What are the implications of her answer? How would you respond to it? Would your response change your reaction within your own office situation? Would you be apt to say something to someone else about it? Would you be likely to be irritable with someone who approaches you at this moment? How could the other secretary have responded to make the situation easier for everyone?

Every job has its tense and harried periods during which you must strive to present a confident, self-assured face to others in the office. Occasionally take a few minutes to relax the muscles and nerves that have been tense under pressure. Emotional moods do not

FIGURE 4-1

go unobserved by other members of the office staff; control yours so that you do not disrupt the work of others.

If your job becomes a continuous ulcer-producing situation in which you find yourself constantly repressing irritability and fighting tenseness, you may need to seek major relief.

Projecting Good Will

Who is the first person a visitor sees when he comes into an office? Who is the first person to whom he speaks?

In any office, the secretary usually meets the visitor before he enters the office of the boss. Since the secretary does represent the boss, it is important to project an attitude of goodwill to the visitor. Usually, it is easy to greet a visitor, but problems do arise. A large number of difficult, awkward situations arise in an office simply because someone on the team flubs human relations. If you consider the types of situations that may occur before you meet them, you can practice various responses to determine the most effective ones. When a problem does arise, it will be difficult enough, but you will be prepared to cope with it.

For example:

One businessman noticed that his visitors all seemed a little less friendly than usual. He was concerned and began to explore the situation. He found that his new secretary was greeting visitors to the office with the curt order, "Have a seat — Mr. Brown will get to you as soon as he can."

A visitor usually feels superior to a secretary and, therefore, resents being ordered to have a seat. Such a response makes him feel frustrated, because, in someone else's office, he can do nothing to correct the situation. In this case, resentment and frustration were reflected in a less-than-friendly attitude toward the boss.

A more pleasant atmosphere could have been achieved had the secretary used a few moments to greet the visitors more warmly. Instead of letting a visitor approach with uncertainty, a secretary should greet him with a smile and a question directed at determining the purpose of his visit. If an appointment has been made, the secretary has information to use in the greeting. As a visitor enters and approaches, the secretary might say, "Mr. Green?" After being assured the visitor is indeed Mr. Green, the secretary might say, "Will you have a seat? Mr. Brown is running a little behind schedule, but I'm sure he will be with you shortly." Or, "Please have a seat. I'll let Mr. Brown know you're here."

It is very disconcerting to visit an office and learn that you must wait — especially when you have an appointment. The visitor considers his time just as valuable as that of your boss. It is also disconcerting to feel that the secretary is delaying letting her boss know that the visitor has arrived for his appointment. The secretary can ease either situation with a little effort. For example, you might say, "A slight emergency has arisen and Mr. Brown is running a few minutes late. May I get you a cup of coffee while you wait?" Or, "Mr. Brown is handling a very serious problem right now — would you mind if I delay announcing you for just a few minutes?" Or, "Mr. Brown is on a long-distance call and should be through shortly. Would you care for a cup of coffee while you wait?"

The secretary is a goodwill ambassador for the boss. This is a vital function of secretarial duties. By projecting a pleasant attitude and a helpful manner, the secretary can be an effective ambassador.

Projecting Self-Control

Perhaps you know someone who always seems to have a smile on his face; this is very important in projecting a pleasant image for the office. Of course, it is more difficult to smile than it is to frown when you are upset or frustrated. But it is so much more effective! Besides, frown lines are unattractive to the personal appearance; smile lines are attractive and friendly.

Have you ever noticed that you are happier when you smile than when you frown? When you are not feeling well, do you smile or do you frown? When you are angry, frustrated, or displeased, do you smile or frown? When you are very pleased, excited, or thrilled, do you smile or frown? Can you turn your feelings around? Do you have enough self-control to conceal your true feelings?

Can you tell how someone else is feeling by the look on his face? If you can develop this perception, you can respond in a more positive way to office visitors and thus become more valuable in your job. Are there those around you who seem capable of camouflaging their feelings so that you are not aware of them? This kind of self-control is very important in developing a good office personality — the art of appearing to be pleasant at all times.

How can such self-control be mastered? Where does the will to exercise this type of control originate? The history of psychology tells us that around 1000 B.C., it was theorized that thought originated in the heart. Today, the common misconception is that emotions are an activity of the heart — it aches, overflows, or becomes like steel. When someone becomes emotional easily, he is described as being "soft-hearted." Yet, in this day of heart-transplant operations, it becomes obvious that a person's emotions do not change when a new heart is inserted into his body. Emotions, then, must originate in another area of the body — perhaps some portion of the brain.

You send messages from the brain to the nerves of your body so that you may feel and thus protect yourself. You send messages to the muscles so that you can handle your body and use it as a functioning machine to do your bidding. It is quite reasonable, therefore, to believe that you can control your emotions by controlling the message center in the brain. It is possible, then, to alter your personality by exercising self-control. You can also alter your personality by exercising absolutely *no* self-control. It is up to you to decide the type of personality you wish to project, then work patiently and constantly to develop it.

Projecting Courtesy

Courtesy is another necessary ingredient to a good office personality. There is nothing special about the courtesy expected in a business office – it is the same ordinary brand of courtesy that is expected of you everywhere. At home, you sometimes show discourtesy and disrespect, and you may get away with it because your family loves you and will put up with a certain amount of it. In a business office, you are expected to be courteous at all times – whether you feel like it or not.

As you become a member of the office team, you will learn that in dealing with visitors to the office you must *always* be courteous. To them, you are a picture of the firm, and the way *you* react is the way the firm will react. There is an old axiom that will be useful to you at times when you feel your halo slipping – "You can catch more flies with honey than with vinegar."

History tells us that when the first telephone exchange was installed in Boston, the operators hired were men. But the men had a tendency to talk back (vinegar) to impatient customers, and this necessitated their replacement by tactful and patient (honey) women. It has recently been determined through surveys that women are more successful bill collectors than men are, because of their ability to perceive and understand problems, and to absorb abusive language and criticism with more flexibility. Figure 4-2 shows typical male and female approaches to the collection of a bill.

Normally, courtesy is not difficult. When you know the basic rules of courtesy, it is not difficult to apply them. How courteous are you, though, when someone does not identify himself on the telephone? When your boss answers the telephone, he wants to know who is on the other end of the line. How do you find out without being discourteous?

For example:

Suppose the secretary buzzes the boss on the intercom, interrupting important thoughts, to announce that a man on line 1 insists on talking to the boss. The boss asks what his name is, and the secretary says she doesn't know – it sounds like Mr. Brown. The boss takes

If we don't receive a check tomorrow, your service will be cut off and your account given to our attorney!

Oh...I understand perfectly. We all get in a tight spot now and then. But it would be a shame to lose your service.. and it does cost the company to continue it

FIGURE 4-2

the call and discovers it is not Mr. Brown at all; it is Mr. White, who should really be speaking with the supervisor in the accounting office.

In this example, the secretary shifted a responsibility to the boss that she should have handled routinely. It shows a lack of responsibility and places the secretary in the position of being criticized for the way the call was handled.

How could the secretary have resolved the situation without interrupting the boss? Even if Mr. White was gruff and discourteous in initiating the call, how could she have handled the situation? If Mr. White failed to respond to any effort of the secretary to obtain his name or elicit the nature of his call, how could she have approached the interruption of the boss so that he would be aware of the need for him to become involved in the call? Was the boss given all the information necessary to let him know that the person on line 1 was uncooperative and insistent? Any office will have its quota of such calls, and it is easier for the boss to handle them if the secretary first fills him in on the nature of the communication up to that point.

The way you answer the telephone will depend upon the way your boss wants you to answer it. There are many accepted variations, such as "Brown & Smith – good morning!" "Brown & Smith, may I help you?" "Brown & Smith, Miss Charming speaking."

When answering the telephone, keep a smile in your voice. The way you say "Hello" becomes much more important on the telephone than in face-to-face communication. Why? Because on the telephone, the listener cannot see you, and must judge you only by the tone of your voice. He will form an image based on voice tone and quality; and his image of you will become his image of your office, and will affect his opinion of your boss, particularly if he does not know him personally.

Once you have answered the phone, you must listen and respond to the caller. Now, suppose the caller says, "Is Mr. Brown in?" What do you say? Remember – Mr. Brown wants you to tell him who is on the line. "Who is calling?" sounds rude and discourteous. It also sounds as if Mr. Brown is having you screen his calls, and the caller may feel that Mr. Brown is unapproachable. This is not the impression the boss wishes to make. "Yes, he is – may I tell him who is calling?" sounds much more courteous and friendly.

You will come to appreciate the person who always identifies himself when he calls on the telephone. Others are not so courteous. There was, for example, the man who replied to the question, "May I tell him who is calling?" with a flat, "Yes, you may."

You will learn to recognize voices of frequent callers, and it is flattering to the caller to be recognized immediately. If you think you know who is calling but are not quite sure, how can you find out without embarrassing either yourself or the caller? Think about various ways of putting words together.

Suppose the caller sounds angry or upset? You must learn to judge when you might be able to soothe the ruffled feelings of the caller, and when you should immediately connect the caller with the boss with no questions asked. Suppose the boss is not in when you get a caller who is angry or upset. Would you promise to have the boss call as soon as he comes in? If so, you might find yourself in a touchy situation with your boss. You can give him a message — you can tell him that he had a call — you can explain the circumstances — but you cannot make him carry out *your* promises.

Should you say, "May I have him call you?" No — because this sounds as if you are promising that the boss will call because you tell him to. Then what *should* you say? Again, there are any number of ways of putting words together. Try a few of these to get you started:

"I'll tell him you called and are anxious to speak with him."

"I'll give him your message. I'm sure he will call just as soon as he can."

"I'll give him the message just as soon as he comes in."

"I'll put a telephone message on his desk right now."

Whatever you do, stay objective about the problem the caller has in getting in touch with your boss. Be sympathetic to his desires and helpful in recording his message, but remain loyal to your boss. There are sometimes circumstances surrounding a call that you cannot reveal, or perhaps do not even know. In either event, you must remember never to sympathize with the caller to the extent of indicating you think your boss has been negligent in any way.

Using Imagination and Initiative

If you deal with people as people, you should be successful in your human relations in the office. There will be very few days, however, that will not hold at least one situation that is awkward in some respect. Sometimes this awkward situation will arise at home, sometimes in the office, sometimes over the telephone, sometimes in your social life. Call upon the experience you have already developed in handling such situations, and then expand your abilities to cover other situations.

What causes an awkward situation? Who is responsible for it? How can you use your imagination and initiative to minimize the emotional trauma arising from an awkward situation?

No one can tell you how, when, or why an awkward situation will develop. Neither can anyone tell you how to react to overcome an aura of unpleasantness. You will develop your own methods and techniques, and your success in dealing with it will depend in part upon your personality.

To be realistic, along with all the wonderful bosses in this world, there are also a very large number of not-so-wonderful bosses. These people are not so impossible to work for, however, if the secretary handles human relations properly. Let's look at some of the awkward situations that arise between a boss and a secretary.

> There was the boss who had a habit of tweaking a secretary's ear. A secretary new to the firm, unaware of this habit, was quite shocked when this happened to her. Naturally, the rest of the office staff was watching to see how she would react to it. She said nothing of the incident to anyone. The next day, the boss asked her to come in for dictation. Very calmly, and without a word to anyone, she reached into her desk drawer, took out a newly purchased pair of earmuffs, set them firmly in place, and entered his office.

This action may seem a bit drastic — the use of such techniques would undoubtedly depend on the ability of the secretary to carry it off with humor. It would also depend on the ability of the boss to accept the action of the secretary in such a way that he would not be embarrassed before the rest of the office staff.

What about awkward situations that occur between you and another secretary? Suppose the secretary near you constantly interrupts your work to ask you how to spell words; and suppose, although you have been quite obliging, you have reached the point of wanting her to stop interrupting you so much. One secretary, finding herself in this situation, solved it by presenting her tormentor with a dictionary. To her surprise, the woman was delighted to receive the book, because she had not been provided with one.

Then there is the office criticizer. This is the person who is quite free in criticizing the way everyone else does things. How do you handle such a situation? Anyone who constantly criticizes others is quite possibly a very insecure person, or one who believes that only criticism will cause others to do a good job.

If you find yourself involved in a conversation with someone who is criticizing either you or another person, you might try to ease the flow by asking, "What would you have done?" or, "How would you have handled it?" and then really listening to the response. If the situation starts to become tense, try to relieve it, but excuse yourself before becoming emotionally involved. Your sense of humor is your best defense against emotional involvement. Find something funny about the situation to allow you to remain objective.

What would you do if you found yourself being asked questions by an office worker who seemed to be trying to obtain information that does not concern him? As you think about this, remember that you want to maintain good human relations. One of the most effective ways of discouraging questions is to turn the question on the individual asking it. For example:

> Suppose you are having a cup of coffee with a fellow worker, and he asks in a conspiratorial tone, "Do you think Mr. Brown is going to fire Bill?" Now, you may know that your boss is not happy with Bill, but you also know you should not discuss this information with anyone. You can turn this question back on him by saying, "Do *you* think he will?" If the questioner persists with, "Well, I thought *you* might know," you can again reveal nothing by saying something like, "Oh, should I? Well, I guess we'll just have to wait and see."

The most important thing to remember is that in handling an awkward situation, you must never resort to untruths or half-truths. Maintain your integrity, assert your loyalty, adhere to your ethics, be courteous, use your imagination and initiative, and you can handle any situation. When you compromise any one of your principles, you will find your ability to handle the situation weakened.

Projecting a Cooperative Attitude

You are employed to perform a specific function of the office. Yet when you see that someone else is in a jam, do you volunteer to help? If someone has a rush job to get out, do you help him? Do you wait to be asked, or do you volunteer? Do you help cheerfully? Are you willing to work overtime if necessary to complete the work? Do you expect to have each favor returned in kind?

The answers you give to the questions above will indicate the feeling you have for teamwork to achieve office production, and the feeling you have for yourself and your own particular function. The way you respond to the needs of others will determine to a great degree their response to your needs, through the principle of reciprocal behavior.

Everyone likes the person who, without being asked, joins in the task to be completed.

> One school administrator had a mailing to get out, and the secretary received permission from a professor to use a few members of her class to help collate the material. They worked well, but by the end of the period the job was still not finished. The secretary was left alone. As she continued to work, a professor started through the room, whistling softly as he went. Without a pause, he noticed her dilemma, joined her and helped finish the job, then went on his way, still whistling.

Do you feel certain jobs are beneath your dignity as a secretary? Do you expect the cleaning staff to adequately dust and clean your boss's desk? Will you check each morning to make sure that his desk is spotless and ready for him? Do you check his supplies, so that he is never caught short? Do you keep his pencils sharp, his pen filled with ink? If he likes fresh coffee, can you make it and serve it? Do you mind checking his desk at the close of the day to make sure that it is neat and ready for the next day? If these jobs are beneath your dignity, then you are not ready for the job.

If you join into the office activity with goodwill and happy spirits — if you can pinch hit for the receptionist, help the mail clerk, run material on the mimeograph when the duplicating clerk is overloaded — you will, because of this type of personality, become a real part of the team.

Suggested Projects

Get in touch with your local telephone company and ask about the use of the teletrainer unit. If possible, keep the unit for several class periods in order that each member of the class may have an opportunity to practice telephone courtesy.

Invite a representative of the telephone company to lecture on telephone courtesy. Present to the representative some of the situations discussed in this chapter, to give an idea of the type of coverage you would like to have in the lecture.

Set up a role-playing situation. Ask several professors and/or administrators to join the class. Let them be the visitors to the office, to be greeted by the receptionist or secretary. Explain what you are trying to achieve, so that they can bring something beneficial to the class. Select two class members to be the receptionist and secretary. The professor may act the role of the boss. Ask the participants to discuss the way class members handled their roles.

Ask your professor to set up a series of awkward situations for you to solve. Try to determine strengths and weaknesses.

Develop
Communication
Skills

Effective communication requires the combined efforts of two people, whether it is being effected on a one-to-one or one-to-forty basis. If one of them has communications difficulty, then the channel through which communication is conducted is as closed as a dead phone line; and the person who claims to have no difficulty in communications may be the one causing the most problems.

Much has been written on communications, and a quick trip to the library can result in the selection of numerous books on the subject. These should be read and reread, for each one has a valuable contribution to make.

This chapter will deal only briefly with each of three areas of communications. Explore other texts and other authors on the subject, and experiment with some of the new communications devices that are available.

ORAL COMMUNICATION

"I can talk to people — I've been doing that all my life."

"I just can't talk to people. I don't know why."

"I don't like to talk to people — I can't seem to get my ideas across."

"I don't have anything important to say."

Do any of these statements fit you? If not, write down a statement that does express the way you feel about oral communication.

Sender–Receiver

In oral communication, there must be a sender (speaker) and a receiver (listener). The speaker sends a message in an attempt to transmit a thought or idea to the listener. If the message is a good one, the listener will receive the same message the sender is projecting — if the listener is a good listener. However, if the message is not clear, the listener will receive a distorted message; or if he is not a good listener, he may misinterpret the message.

The fortunate thing about face-to-face oral communication is that it is possible to watch facial reactions, and this helps to determine if the message is being received properly. If it is apparent that there is confusion (a frown, a raised eyebrow, a smirk), then the speaker can immediately send a second message to clarify the first: "What I mean is . . ." But even on the telephone, if the listener does not quite grasp the message, he can immediately ask questions to clarify the speaker's idea: "Let me see if I understand you correctly. You are saying . . . ," or, "Did I understand you to say . . . ," or, "You mean if . . ." If the listener fails to ask questions, he is not fulfilling his role in oral communication.

Interest-Centered Communication

Watch oral communication in action around the lunch table. If there isn't much to talk about, the conversation will lag; but if someone has a juicy bit of gossip, watch the ears prick up and attention focus on the speaker. In watching carefully, you may miss out on the gossip item, but you will learn a lesson about communication and people's actions when there are items of talk they do not particularly wish to hear, versus their reactions to items they are eager to hear.

Human nature decrees that we usually hear what we want to hear, not necessarily what the speaker wants us to hear. This trait sometimes produces a kink in the communications lines and can cause confusion, misunderstanding, and frustration.

People have a tendency to want to be the sender rather than the receiver, for it is easier to talk than to listen. But there is no communication without a receiver. A receiver that is corked is no receiver at all. If your telephone line were dead, would you attempt to complete your call? If your human receiver is corked in face-to-face communication, that communication can be no better than it would be over the dead telephone line. The cork must be removed before a successful communication can be effected.

Dialect and Slang

Do you have trouble sending messages?

Do you have difficulty receiving messages?

Do you speak with a regional or foreign accent?

Do you use a large number of slang words — words that may not be understood by the listener?

Do you have a problem understanding dialect of one type or another?

If the answer to any of these questions is "Yes," be very careful that your message is clear to the listener, and his to you. To do this may require that you put additional effort into learning to express yourself more effectively by using the conventional terms used in the community.

When you are the listener, you listen in two ways: (1) in terms of your own experiences, and (2) in terms of the dictionary meaning of words. If a person uses words with which you are unfamiliar, do you ask for clarification? Do you try to extend your vocabulary so that your listening techniques are perfected? Do you find it easy or difficult to understand a person with an accent, whether foreign or regional? Words are pronounced differently in various parts of the United States.

The capital of Peru is pronounced "LEE-ma"; but the natives of Lima, Ohio, pronounce the name of their city "LYE-ma." For the word "hardly," Bostonians say "hadly," and Texans "hahdly."

Lazy Speech

Suppose someone says, "I ast him to go with me." Do you recognize that as being the same as, "I asked him to go with me"? What about the sentence, "I wisht I had it." Do you recognize this as, "I wish I had it"? Sentences are understandable in verbal terms that might be confusing in written terms. Lazy habits of speech or variations in dialect can be handled on a verbal level, but the written word of formal business-letter writing or business-report writing should reflect no dialect or lazy habits of grammar.

Different words are used in various parts of the country to name things. For example, a "river" in some parts of the country may be a "run" in another part. A "creek" (small river) may be called a "crik." A paper bag may be referred to as a "poke," or a "sack."

Attentive Receiver

To be a good listener requires that you identify, as you listen, exactly what idea the speaker is trying to convey. Sometimes, particularly when we are pressured to finish a report or when we have something to decide, we become rather frustrated in our attempt to interpret what is being said, and we do not listen as closely as we should. Under such conditions, poor communication invariably results.

Some people communicate at a faster pace than do others. A good speaker and a good listener achieve rapid communication, and that communication is usually accurate. If either one involved in the process is slow, the entire communication is slower — hence the time needed for good communication is greater. It is important, therefore, to improve your ability to communicate orally as either speaker or listener, in order that the flow of work in the office may proceed as rapidly as possible.

When you don't particularly want to hear a message, you tend to tune out. "I wish you would clean up your room" can be easily tossed off by the teenager, who couldn't care less about the appearance of the room. But "Clean up your room or you cannot use the car tonight" is not so easily tossed off, because it contains two messages, one of which is important to the teenager and is also contingent upon the action called for in the other message. Which of the following has more meaning for the secretary?

"I need that letter as soon as possible."

"That letter must be in the mail today, even if you must stay overtime."

In response to the question, "Why do you want this job?" which of the following responses would be most effectively received by the employer?

"Well, I'm out of school and I need to go to work, I guess."

"I've been looking forward to putting my skills to work, and I think your company is a good place for employment. I believe I would enjoy working here, and I think I have the qualifications for the job."

The impression of the first response would probably be negative. It says to the employer, "I don't really want this job, or any other for that matter." The second response is geared directly to the question and would create a favorable impression.

The important thing to be remembered is that communication always takes place — the question is whether that communication is effective. Does it accomplish what it is intended to accomplish?

Communication Breakdown

Let's look at a few examples of communication.

A young woman entered a hospital but refused to sign the surgical release. The named operation had not been discussed with her, and, in fact, was not compatible with her conversations with her doctor. She entered the hospital room and, after looking at the patient chart, said to one of the medical aids, "The doctor's name on my chart is not that of my doctor." The aide replied, "Is that so? Well, don't worry about it — we process so many patients, and when you have a lot of people coming in, it is easy to make an error."

Analyze that communication. What is wrong with it? How does it miscommunicate? If it is so easy to make an error about a doctor's relationship to a patient, how easy is it to make an error in medication? How easy is it to perform the wrong surgery — or prepare a patient for the wrong surgery? Realizing that mistakes can be made, how much more effective would the communication have been if the aide had said, "Well, we'd better check that right now and see that all of our records are correct. Who *is* your doctor?"

Why do communications break down? Primarily, because people fail to think before speaking about the effect their words will have. If a person thinks about the impact his words will have on the receiver, his communication will be more effective. Is the message one the receiver will be pleased to hear? If so, communication will be relatively easy. Is the message one the receiver will be reluctant to accept? If so, the message must be especially well worded.

A well-planned presentation is always more effective than a spontaneous one. In ordinary conversation, however, planning must take place as the conversation progresses, thus requiring each individual to be alert to the immediate impact of words, ready to correct any impression that might be detrimental to the true intent of a communication.

> An employee calls the receptionist at 8:30 A.M. and leaves the message, "I will be late because I made a doctor's appointment for this morning at 10:30." Now, at 9:30, the boss wants to speak with this particular employee. The receptionist delivers the message.

What will the employer think? Will he think that the employee should bear in mind certain obligations to the company to make doctor's appointments on his own time? Is there anything in the message that would indicate an emergency of some nature? In a communication such as this, the employer has only the cold factual words of the message — without benefit of the tone of voice or the inflection put upon words.

Communications Assistance

In face-to-face situations, oral communication consists of more than just words — facial expressions become a factor in conveying meaning. The words may sound harsh, but facial expression (body language) may modify the harshness and reduce the sting. On the other hand, the words may be rather mild, but the facial expression can emphasize the seriousness of the meaning. Tone of voice places emphasis on certain words, and thus becomes important in conveying the meaning of a communication. A stamp of the foot, a wink of the eye, a muscle twitch — all convey certain meanings.

Oral communication other than face to face, such as telephone conversation, is limited primarily to word usage and tone of voice.

You cannot see the other person respond, and therefore you must depend on the stimulus-response method until you get certain responses indicating that the message has been accurately given and received.

Vocabulary

Some people are more adept than others at the use of words. One need not have an extensive vocabulary to be an effective communicator, but the vocabulary should be large enough for the word usage to be varied. An occasional large word is effective in communication, but constant use of three-and four-syllable words sounds affected and snobbish, and may result in negative responses that are triggered by a resentment of the work involved in receiving the message. If there is need for a large word, use it. If there is no such need, a small one will do as well to convey a specific meaning. Be conscious, however, of using a word so much that you wear it out. When that begins to happen, study your dictionary or thesaurus and find a substitute to use occasionally.

Private Communications

It is possible to communicate too frequently. It must be remembered that during office hours, the employee owes his prime attention to the work to be accomplished. Private conversations, both face to face and on the telephone, should be reserved for your own time – coffee breaks, lunchtime, or after hours. When it is necessary to make or receive a telephone call, keep it as brief as possible. Even though work may have slowed briefly for you, someone may be placing a call to your office, and a constant busy signal is frustrating. If your boss is out of the office, he may be trying to call you. Keep the lines as free as possible.

Clear Communications Lines

Your primary function as a secretary will be in the area of communications. You will be dealing with communications both oral and written. Superior secretaries are experts in communications. Learn to select words that convey exact meanings. Learn to listen accurately. Master tact, diplomacy, and self-control in the area of communications. Above all else, be able to admit (1) that you may not have conveyed a clear message, and (2) that you may not have interpreted a message accurately. With an open mind, you can recommunicate more effectively. Understanding that you may have erred in communication, you can understand that others may also err. Occasionally a "storm" attacks communications lines, sometimes resulting in total destruction; so try to keep the kinks out of the lines. Every once in a while, tighten up a line by having a heart-to-heart talk with the person with whom you are having the most communications difficulties. In this way, your communications network is always open to send or to receive messages.

WRITTEN COMMUNICATION

The English language offers a challenge to the secretary. Good courses in basic business English or in report writing are invaluable. Sometimes, in the educational process, literature has been stressed and the student develops a "literary style," inappropriate for effective business communication. Can you imagine a message directed to call people to a staff meeting, which reads:

Prithee, your presence is requested in yon Conference Room at half-past one.

or:

Your boss would be honored to receive you in the Conference Room at half-past the hour of one for the purpose of discussing some matters of importance.

In the business world, the message would be constructed briefly and to the point:

Staff meeting: Conference Room, 1:30 Wednesday

People have enough trouble with language without compounding it with excess verbiage. There was, for example, a vivacious little woman who had spent a number of years in Brazil, speaking only Portugese. Returning to her native English language, she said, "I don't like elevators because I get hydrophobia." She had had similar trouble one day in Brazil, when she selected the wrong Portugese term and instructed a maintenance man to "fly the bathtub on top of the new flagpole."

Meanings must be made clear if the written communication is not to be subject to interpretation. The secretary's prime function in written communication is to check each sentence for clarity and correctness — even if it means slight alterations to dictated material.

Dictated Messages

Many secretaries consider so sacred every word the boss utters that they are afraid to make even slight alterations. Although there are a few bosses who believe they have a complete command of the language (and some really do) and therefore insist upon no changes, most bosses will welcome the secretary who can help make their communications clear and meaningful. Sweeping changes would be insulting to the dictator, but minor alterations may be necessary. The prime concern in making alterations of any nature is to assure that the meaning has not been changed in the process; therefore, changes in wording or punctuation should be brought to the attention of the boss for his approval.

The secretary should realize that her boss may not be a paragon in the spelling area, either. He would far rather have the secretary correct his spelling than be embarrassed by having an error called to his attention by a peer or a superior. Therefore, if you are typing from a rough draft, correct any and all spelling errors. If you are typing from dictated copy, the complete responsibility for spelling is yours. Remember, it is embarrassing for the boss, and it probably would embarrass you, to have spelling errors discovered *after* material has left your office.

Use the Dictionary.   Learn to use your dictionary effectively, because when the boss dictates a word that is unfamiliar to you, you will need to check its spelling and meaning. How do you begin to look up an unfamiliar word? Why don't you use the dictionary as a "browsing" book? When you have a few spare moments, open it at random, glance down the columns of words, and read one or two that are not familiar to you. This will increase your reading and listening vocabulary and, at the same time, help you recognize sounds in various words. When you hear a strange word, write it down phonetically (by sound) and then look it up in the dictionary. Seek help if you need it, but don't give up until the word is found.

Study Writing Style. As you type dictated material, study the style of writing. Everyone has pet phrases he tends to use frequently, unique ways of putting words together to convey specific meanings, and a certain style in the selection of words. Remember, written communications require careful handling, because their meaning depends on the visualization of words on paper — there is nothing else to convey the meaning. If the writer and the reader are personally acquainted, communication becomes a little easier, but a large margin for error still exists. Word choice, phrasing patterns, spelling, and punctuation all become extremely important in putting sentences together in a business letter. Your contribution to the written word will be easier and more acceptable in your office if you can pick up the style of your boss.

If you can master his style of writing, you can be most helpful in written communications by taking care of certain more or less routine kinds of correspondence for the boss. Your assumption of this responsibility will free him to turn his attention to the more important items of communication.

Learn Industry's Terminology. Society seems to be making up words faster than the dictionary publishers can keep up with them. Many of the words will be unique to the business in which your firm is engaged. Develop a dictionary of business terminology geared to your industry — words not necessarily found in the conventional dictionary, but most effective in conveying messages within the industry. Your principal function here becomes one of judgment when you are typing a communication. If a letter is going to the outside world — out of the industry — conventional words should be used, and you may need to alter the communication to assure that the message will not frustrate the receiver; this is a grave responsibility, for the meaning must not be changed.

Composing Communications

Secretaries who compose memorandums and letters for the signature of the boss assume the responsibility of clear and meaningful communications. It does make a difference, for example, whether a telephone number is typed 820-300 or 820-3000.

> A clerical error was made at the telephone company when a customer had a change in service. The error was made in the spelling of a surname and caused the loss of the transfer of calls to the new number. It continued for months, until the customer had occasion to find that long-distance friends were unable to get the new number from the telephone company.

The error consisted of two letters, which had been reversed in typing the customer's name. The result was a different name. It made a difference to the customer involved, to the people trying to call the customer, and to the telephone company when they had to adjust the bill for services not rendered.

Proofread.   Errors such as the one discussed above are usually the result of lazy habits of proofing typed copy. It is easy but expensive to drift into lazy habits, and the secretary must guard against carelessness on the job.

Frequently, a secretary is faced with a correspondence situation in which the same letter, with only minor variations, could go to ten different people; and all ten letters could be effective. It is in this type of situation that the most extreme caution should be used.

> A secretary working for an insurance firm had written numerous letters following up on the payment of claims of one kind or another. All the letters were similar in nature, but one was a drastic mistake. Writing to a policyholder who had just lost her husband and collected on his life insurance policy, the secretary wrote, ". . . . We are happy we could be of service to you, and hope we can serve you in a similar capacity again."

Use Reference Books.   When you are composing communications, good reference books are invaluable. Consult them frequently — they are friends. Some secretaries hide their dictionaries and reference manuals and use them surreptitiously. No one expects you to know everything! The boss will respect you for using reference books of all types and will probably be glad to purchase them if you ask. Naturally, a boss would not expect you to look up every other word — but sometimes even that is necessary when you are dealing with extremely technical material.

How do you convey the importance of a telephone message or a message left for the boss? The urgency of each message should be identified; and the most urgent given to the boss first. The invention of the telephone message pad — a typical example is shown in Figure 5-1 — has been a boon to the secretary, but it is not always used efficiently. After checking off the items on the message sheet, you will frequently find it necessary to add a written note. Strive to make that note brief, but absolutely clear. In completing the message to

To ——————————————————————

Date ———————————— Time ——————

MESSAGE

Name ——————————————————————

Phone ——————————————————————

Please Call	
Returned Your Call	
Will Call Again	
Would Like An Appointment	

Message ——————————————————————

————————————————————————

————————————————————————

————————————
Message Taken By

FIGURE 5-1

be delivered, it is far too easy to omit an item of information when recording the message. Therefore, a word of caution is in order: Fill in each blank, including date, time, and phone number, as you take the message over the telephone. Never recopy a message. Whether a note is added or not, sign the message slip.

The effectiveness of the secretary in communicating will depend on his educational background and his command of the English language. No matter how good you are, you can be better. You will make mistakes, but you can improve.

READING

Yes, reading is a communications tool. All correspondence is subject to interpretation of the reader — otherwise, why write? The ability of the reader to correctly interpret the message is of prime importance to communications effectiveness. A communications gap between the writer and the reader results in frustration and mis-understanding, and sometimes contributes to loss of business.

Broaden Business Knowledge

The secretarial role in reading is obviously to interpret the message the boss is trying to communicate and to preserve or to clarify it so that the reader receives a clear, concise, not-to-be-misunderstood message. To do this, the secretary must broaden his own knowledge about the industry in which he works. He must know the terminology unique to the industry and he must understand certain policies and positions on company business. He must gain these understandings through talking to his boss, through discussions and conferences (by listening), and through extensive reading. He must develop perception.

Make note of which magazines your boss reads, and use this as a beginning reading list. Explore the company library, or engage in some employee-employer discussions on periodicals of the business world. Browse through bookstands for business magazines.

"How dull?" — not at all! — "How exciting!" If you have a goal in reading, reading becomes exciting. You will be reading because you believe there is something to be gained. No one is standing over you telling you how much or what kind of reading to do. You select the articles you read and the time you wish to spend in such reading. The real pleasure comes when you gain enough background to become perceptive to situations in which you can start putting your new found knowledge to work.

Improve Your Reading Rate

If you feel your reading rate is a little too slow for comfort, try a few experiments to increase your reading skills. Pick up the newspaper; it contains new material each day. Select an item that holds some interest for you — judge from the headline. News columns are just right for speed-reading techniques to be used; the narrow column keeps you from moving your eyes across the page. Focus on the middle of the column and use your peripheral vision to see the ends of the column. Then, instead of reading from left to right, try reading a whole line at a time, and read straight *down* the column. Don't stop your eye movement until you reach the end of the column, then stop, close your eyes, and think about what you absorbed. If you must, reread the column more slowly. If you did a good job the first time, try another column, but this time increase the downward speed — absorb, rather than read each word.

While you are in school, ask your professor to make available to you some time on a controlled-reading machine. This machine can actually time your reading and can force your reading rate upward if you will use it consistently. Many business professors use such a machine in teaching skill subjects, so it may be readily available.

You will read faster only when you want to and when you are convinced that you need to read faster. Practice is the key. Never forget, however, that it is the content of the message that is important — so when you are reading for content you may need to study the material more closely than you would otherwise. You may also be surprised to find that you grasp more of the meaning when you read at the faster pace than at the slower pace.

Setting Priorities

If you are charged with opening the mail for the boss and preparing it in priority for handling, your reading becomes significantly more important. The message in each piece of mail must be interpreted and evaluated by you and placed in some priority order.

Priorities become very significant when deadlines are involved. Again, a certain amount of perception is necessary for decision making, and this perception is developed through working with the employer.

Reading for Clarity

As you type correspondence, your reading rate is important. A fast reader becomes a faster typist, but you must also read for continuity, clarity, and good human relations. Proofreading is absolutely essential to meaningful correspondence — proofread for typing errors, for spelling errors, for errors in grammar, and for errors in statements made in the correspondence.

Statements may be made in many ways. Suppose you read the sentence:

> It was reported that your store was destroyed by fire by our salesman.

What conclusion might you draw? Is there another way to read the sentence? Did the salesman report the fire, or did he set fire to the store? The way a sentence is stated very definitely affects the way a person will read it. Each sentence should stand alone — separate and independent of any other sentence.

How do you read the following sentence?

> I shall await your check in the enclosed envelope.

Where are you? Are you in the envelope? Reword the sentence so that the reader will receive the correct message.

Try this sentence:

> Miss Rose Smith did work in my office during the summer, and when she quit to return to college, I was fully satisfied.

Poor Miss Smith! Can you reword the sentence to reflect to the reader that Miss Smith did a good job while she was working in the office?

Now that you have mastered that sentence, try this one:

> Being marked down to half price, I am sure you can understand our position.

How do you interpret that sentence? Do you feel elated at being marked down? Just what are you worth? Can you untangle the sentence so that the reader will not be confused?

THE COMMUNICATIONS EXPERT

There is a tendency in the business world to "pass the buck," because human nature involves ego. As a secretary, you can't afford an ego. By the very nature of things, you will find that all communications errors fall on your shoulders, so expect it and accept it.

As a secretary, you must know about the business of your office, you must keep tabs on deadlines, you must make sure that appointments are made and kept promptly. You must become an expert in all communications media. When you accept this responsibility, you can brighten the picture for yourself as an expert in communications — oral, written, or read. You can improve your own techniques of communication and find a happier life in the process.

Suggested Projects

Ask your professor to obtain the record or tape of "Effective Listening," by Dr. Ralph Nichols, published by Xerox, and listen to it either in groups or individually.

Locate some type of controlled-reading machine and determine your reading speed. Use it individually to improve your reading skill.

Using a tape recorder, record several messages as you would if you were charged with giving each message to someone else. Analyze your oral communications by listening to the tape. Ask your professor for advice on how to improve.

Invite your college president to lecture on the "Art of Communication."

Your professor has given you a test to prepare. You had two pages typed and a third in the typewriter when it became urgent that you leave your desk. When you returned, you noticed a certain rearrangement of the material, which caused you to believe someone had been at your desk. Think about what may have happened and react to the situation.

6

Develop A Personal Relationship With the Boss

If a boss could run his office alone, he would have no need for employees. Of course, the employees follow his leadership, direction, or orders; but *what* they do is not as important as *the way in which they do it*. Employees can do much to increase the production of the office, and production is what most interests the boss. Ask most employees what relationship they have with their boss, and the most common answer will be, "He is the boss and I do what he tells me to do. That is our relationship." An employee who thinks like this has, at best, a mediocre relationship with the boss, in which two-way communication is virtually impossible.

Human relations and psychology classes stress the theory that if you help push someone up the ladder of success, he will pull you up behind him. Therefore, the sooner you start to push your boss, the sooner he will be able to pull you up with him. Before this theory can operate, however, you will find a need for some basic, fundamental understandings between the secretary and the boss.

NEED FOR FUNDAMENTAL UNDERSTANDINGS

One of the understandings needed between the employer and the employee is that of how much assistance the employer needs to climb the success ladder. Of course, this also depends on how much the employer can trust you to accept certain responsibilities; therefore, building this understanding will take time.

There are also personal matters that must be understood between the boss and the secretary. It is difficult for a man to open a discussion of a rather personal nature with a woman without seeming to be personally and romantically aggressive, or excessively critical; it is difficult for a woman executive to open a discussion of a personal nature with a secretary of either sex without projecting an image of prudishness or of maternalism. They must recognize each other as human beings and build a solid relationship based on adult mutual respect. They must understand together that feelings of ill temper, anger, frustration, and the like must be understood and recognized for what they are if a productive relationship is to be built.

When you read a novel, don't you tend to classify it by the amount of personal involvement you feel as you read? What causes you to become personally involved in a novel? Isn't it characters who are whole, rounded people, with all the virtues and flaws real people have? A series of situations involving conflict of varying kinds? Relationships among the characters that lead to the development of plot? A setting that departs from the humdrum and everyday?

If this is true, then you can understand that an office in which an "Elsie Dinsmore" atmosphere prevails, with everything going smoothly all the time because "Papa Boss" makes all the decisions, can be a dull place in which to work. On the other hand, the office that has a *Gone With the Wind* type of human relationships keeps interest and production going in every direction of effort. A healthy human relationship leads to altercations, misunderstandings, and all types of emotional involvement. Together, the boss and the secretary have the choice of working individually in a safe relationship, or together in a productive team effort.

DEVELOPING A TEAM RELATIONSHIP

What is a team? Why is a team effort needed? How do you put together a productive team? Look at these questions and analyze them in terms of your own background.

What is a team? Simply defined, a team is two or more people working together to achieve a common goal. A team can be composed of as few as two people or of as many as thousands — such as an armed force. Therefore, a team may be very small or very large. There may be a team within a team, and this is true in the larger and more complex units. In a large company, for example, all employees are considered to be on the company team; but there are many offices and divisions that are teams of their own. In office situations, the employees must learn where and how their own team unit functions as a segment of the larger team.

Why is a team effort needed? Can you imagine a marriage being successful if the couple does not establish or identify their "team relationship" so that the two of them work for the same goals? What would happen if each went his own way with no regard for the other? How successful would a football team be if each member went his own way? How successful would a pilot be, flying from one side of the continent to another, without the teams on the ground to help him? For that matter, how successful would the pilot be without the team that flies with him? The size of the team is determined by the size of the job to be done. But no matter how small the team, team effort is needed, even while individual characteristics are also needed to put spark and life in the team relationships.

How do you put together a productive team? That is indeed the problem faced by executives every day. After reviewing the application and studying the credentials of an applicant, and after interviewing those who seem best qualified for the job, the executive makes a selection and hopes his decision has been wise. Each week and each month, with each change in the company, the composition of the team changes somewhat; therefore, the composition is never static — it is constantly being fed new membership. When the team is a good one, the company shows greater success than when the team members fall below the usual standard.

People working together must be concerned with each other and with what happens to them as they work together in the office environment. If the boss has to treat his secretary so carefully that he never steps on her toes, then he cannot be productive. One of the secretary's prime values comes with letting the boss be a human being in the office.

If the boss is a pack-rat type, the secretary should be the opposite — eager to throw things away, to get rid of the nonessential, to keep the files clean. If the boss tends to throw things away quickly with only a glance, the secretary should be careful about throwing things away, screening everything assiduously to be sure of its value. In other words, the secretary should strive to compensate for the weaknesses of the boss.

Forming half of a two-man team, the secretary must fill in the gaps in the boss's job. A good secretary will do as many of the small jobs as possible, to give the boss time to do the larger jobs. If the boss is angry or frustrated, the secretary will try to shield him from visitors until he can regain his composure. If the boss is faced with a deadline, the secretary will keep minor irritations (such as a complaint that can wait another day, or an appointment that can be made for tomorrow) from interfering with his work. The good secretary will understand why the boss is in a particular mood, and will adjust his own work to that mood to create the atmosphere that will be conducive to maintaining a high production level and good personal working relationships.

How to Address the Boss

To start building a personal relationship, find out what the boss wants to be called by you. If his name is Bill and he wants you to call him Bill, then do so. However, when you are talking to others in the office, on the phone, or elsewhere, refer to him as "Mr. Smith" — *always*. Thus, the relationship between you and the boss becomes more personal, but the respect due his position is maintained.

For example, suppose a visitor arrives for an unscheduled visit. After greeting the visitor and finding out the nature of the visit, you go into the office of the boss and say, "Bill, Jim Young would like to see you about a problem in Purchasing." When you return to the outer office, you tell Jim, "Mr. Smith will be out in just a minute."

Writing Style

Each individual has his own style of writing, expressions he uses frequently, phrasing patterns unique to him. The secretary, in helping the boss to be successful, should adopt his letter-writing style. Writing style is a personal characteristic, so to achieve this ability, the secretary must study the boss, talk about certain situations, and even pry into his emotions about some situations. Only in this way can a secretary write a letter that sounds as if it had been dictated by the employer.

Developing Trust

No one can tell you how to develop a personal relationship — it must be sensed. But as a clue in this situation, the boss's work is the secretary's work. They must form a team concentrating on the same goals, the same aims, and the same method of reaching goals.

The secretary must take the initiative of creating an atmosphere of trust. Never betray the trust of your position. You type correspondence, you handle confidential matters, you keep the files — thus you have access to all the activities of the office. The boss has no choice but to trust you. Never betray that trust.

To a large extent, the secretary must dictate to the boss — but always in the privacy of his office. If the boss is extremely busy, he may have only a few minutes a day to take care of some matters. It is the secretary's job to bring the most important items to his attention during this period of time. If the boss is irritated, the secretary must still make sure that he gets the important matters taken care of — even in the face of being criticized at the moment.

COPING WITH CRITICISM

A good personal relationship will cause the secretary to ignore the criticism of the boss if it is given in the process of taking care of important matters. There are times, however, when criticism becomes a problem to an employee, and you must be prepared to cope with it.

You have already learned that there are many kinds of criticism. If you assume the risk of being aggressive and of taking responsibility, you run the risk of getting bawled out occasionally. If you are human, you are bound to make mistakes, and if you make mistakes, you will be criticized. How do you cope with it?

Breaking Down Fears

Why do adults fear to use their imagination or aggressiveness, or to project ideas that would promote productivity? Because of the fear of being reminded of the mistake, or because of the embarrassments that come from being told one went too far, or failed to carry through. So if you can eliminate these fears, you can have the freedom to make waves, to innovate, or to use your imagination.

Throughout history, thinking people have been in competition with each other. Competition brings criticism. Depending on the extent and the results of the criticism, people have reacted in different ways. To some, criticism brings a desire to prove, either to oneself or to others, the accuracy of the idea or thought. To some, criticism kills incentive to devise new ideas or to project such ideas to those who could put them into operation. In the first instance, criticism results in challenge; in the second, criticism results in defeat.

Criticism as a Communications Tool. Criticism comes in various forms. The kind that results in a challenge is helpful criticism — constructive in design, intended to inspire the person to continue to think. Criticism that results in defeat is the kind that is stinging and sometimes unjustified. On the other hand, the way a person takes criticism is an important factor. Criticism, then, is one of the communications tools. Two things are important in thinking about criticism; (1) the meaning of the critic — the intent or purpose of the criticism; and (2) the receptiveness of the individual being criticized — his ability to accept criticism, and the effect such words have on his actions.

Emotional Involvement. No matter how criticism is viewed, by either the critic or the receiver, there is a personal involvement of emotion in the process. It is the control of this emotion that becomes of primary importance during the first moments following a critical remark. How you react will be extremely important in your business life.

What is the best way to cope with criticism? Why, simply to avoid it. Use your initiative. When you know you have erred or failed to carry through on an activity, report immediately to the boss and tell him you are ready for your chewing out — don't wait for him to come to you. If you are clever enough to turn the situation into a humorous one, if you can make the boss smile, it is very difficult for him to become angry. How can you be criticized if you have already admitted your error and criticized yourself before he even discovered it? By criticizing yourself, you retain your self-respect. Give him all the gory details so that there is nothing left to fear. Then tell him what you are doing to rectify your error.

A child can try the patience of his parents until they lose their tempers completely. He can do this because he has yet to form a sense of dignity or pride. The adult, however, is saturated in his sense of dignity and pride, and criticism strikes directly at the quick of this emotion. If you can disarm a potential critic with a funny remark, then you can salvage the situation without the trauma of having the boss criticize your actions.

Undeserved Criticism

There are times when you will be criticized unfairly. How do you think you should cope with such a criticism? You can't hope to cope with the unknown, so the first thing you must do is listen to the criticism — all of it. Ask questions, and if you ask enough questions in an interested, responsible manner, the boss will probably realize that if you are guilty you should know the answers to these questions, and he will wonder why you are asking. You can prove that the criticism is unfair without once issuing an outright denial.

Usually, when you try to deny a charge in the midst of being criticized, your denial sounds false and hollow and creates an embarrassing situation. So keep asking questions, and if the boss doesn't respond to the fact that you are being criticized unfairly, simply apologize and tell him you were completely unaware of having done this and that you certainly will not repeat it. It is far better to take undeserved blame gracefully than to get yourself into an embarrassing situation by becoming defensive with righteous denial. And remember, you are giving the boss the right to be human and make a mistake once in a while.

What would you do if the boss leveled a criticism at you in the presence of someone else? Above all, remember: Do not embarrass your boss! Even though you may feel a certain shock when this happens, you must tickle your brain rapidly and come up with a face-saving idea. Can you make it funny? You might try to pass it off and change the subject without seeming to be rude. Or you might quickly admit that that error really was a classic — one that probably you alone are capable of making. Or if you realize a criticism is imminent, you can begin to walk him away from the group atmosphere — perhaps into his office. Whatever you do, you must create an awareness that this is awkward for all of you without actually saying it. You must be the instrument of saving face for everyone, and you are the only one who can do this. Only if you have a good personal relationship with the boss, and if you know his strengths and weaknesses so that you can use them to your advantage, can you handle such an awkward situation. Furthermore, you should never indicate to anyone that you think your boss was wrong. Simply maintain your poise and refuse to discuss the situation further.

Psychologists tell us that criticism is most damaging when it comes from someone we admire; that is why it is difficult to cope with at the moment it is given.

BECOMING PERCEPTIVE

How do you become so perceptive that you can immediately recognize the correct way to handle awkward situations — such as coping with criticism leveled in the presence of someone else? No one can teach you to be perceptive. How do a husband and wife become perceptive to each other's needs, desires, and moods? The answer is, obviously, by living together. You cannot be perceptive to a stranger. You must build a close relationship, one that is meaningful in the office environment, before you can become perceptive to each other. Naturally, this cannot be accomplished rapidly, nor can it be forced. Two people, working as a team, must develop a close relationship by virtue of working together for common goals. You must make an effort to understand each other; sometimes you must ask personal questions and pry into the reasons for certain reactions or feelings. *You must be able to discuss office situations and problems openly and without fear of intruding on each other's domain.* You must pry into each other's emotions for the purpose of understanding.

Using Initiative

Nothing is more frustrating to a boss than to have the secretary assume rules that actually do not exist. These nonexistent rules can prevent the building of perception and understanding. When you *think* there is a rule, ask yourself these questions: (1) Does this rule really exist, or does it exist only in my mind? (2) Is the rule written down? (3) Did someone tell me about the rule, and, if so, who told me?

If you are still in doubt, ask your boss. If he avoids stating a rule, accept the fact that there is no such rule and stop acting on the assumption that there is — regardless of what anyone else says. Sometimes too much discussion with fellow employees can be detrimental to you. Remember, work primarily with your boss, secondarily with your fellow employees.

Define Your Domain. In using your initiative, you must define the limits of your domain within the office. In the home, the husband and wife usually agree between them who will handle certain matters. One or the other of them pays the bills, shops for groceries, buys the clothing and other personal needs of the family, or earns the income. In the office, similar domains exist. One of the two-man team mans the filing system, writes the letters, greets visitors to the office, makes minor decisions, and makes major decisions. Each boss and secretary must define their own particular domains as they learn to work together in a close personal relationship. What will work for one situation will very probably fail in another.

Before you can really use your initiative in handling situations, you must feel sure of your limits, and only you and your boss can define these limits. When you are trying to define them, you will both make mistakes. In fact, it is a good idea to make a few mistakes deliberately. Get into trouble early on the job. Only by getting into trouble can you define the limits. As you press to find limits, you will find yourself using your initiative. Follow the pattern a child follows —he goes as far as he can until Father puts his foot down.

Rule Your Domain.   The office filing system probably creates more doubts about rules than does any other office function. Being new on the job, you open that three- or four-drawered monstrosity and look at the mass hidden inside. You immediately think of the many ways your professors taught you to file — yet this looks utterly foreign and somehow sacred. It creates its own fears within you. Do you dare make any changes? If you do make changes, will you lose something? How can you be sure you can locate what the boss wants? What are the rules about the office files? Rules – rules – rules!

Relax! What rules? Was this system set up as an organizational system, or did someone put these files together? Are there *really* any rules? Who is responsible for these files now? For what purpose do they exist? Having answered these questions, remember that this is *your* domain. The boss depends on you to file material and to retrieve it when he needs it. He probably couldn't care less whether you file a letter under "L" for letter, "P" for paper, or "M" for mail. The only thing he really cares about is that you can find it when he needs it. Therefore, unless the organization specifies a filing system, any rule made concerning filing will be *your* rule. So take the initiative and rule over your domain.

As you take this initiative, you must remember that there will be days when you will be absent from the office, out for a coffee break, or on an errand when the boss wants something from the file. It will be necessary for someone else to find the item in question. As you design your own filing system, you should record that system — perhaps in a "File Guide," to be kept in a folder at the front of the first drawer of the filing cabinet for easy reference, or perhaps recorded in your secretarial *Reference Manual*, which is readily available on your desk. Inform your boss and another secretary where to find your "File Guide" and how to use it, in the event that they need to make reference to your files.

Get away from self-imposed limitations. They are hard to fight when you are trying to gain the productivity needed in the office, or when you need to use your imagination to get a job done efficiently. Rules grow like rumors. Don't let them hamper you. When you need a rule, your boss will make sure you know about it — you needn't manufacture one yourself.

LEARN YOUR JOB

There are certain kinds of information that every secretary should be given during the first few days on a new job. As simple as this information is, it is surprising how often it is not supplied. Most management-level jobs have a job-description sheet detailing the requirements and expectations of jobs at that level; and yet, most companies fail to prepare a job-description sheet for the secretarial and clerical jobs. The secretary is brought into the office, introduced to several of the other secretaries, assigned a desk and typewriter, shown where the supplies are, and turned loose to do his job. Perhaps the reason for this is that an efficient secretary follows instructions so well and completes tasks so unquestioningly that many employers fail to give full recognition to the amount and volume of work required on specific secretarial jobs. As the day-to-day routine is established, the boss takes for granted the work of the secretary, for the secretary rarely complains, knowing that what the boss wants done must be done.

If you find yourself in a job that provides no job description or procedures manual, start building your own. Write down every new type of duty that you are instructed to perform. Daily, record information that you need but that was not provided to you at the time of your employment. As you elicit the information you need, record its source for future reference.

Some of the information that you will need to have is listed below:

Names of fellow workers
Names of superiors with whom you will be in contact
How the telephone should be answered
Preferred format for memorandums, letters, envelopes
How and where to obtain supplies
Machines to be operated
  Instructions, if necessary
  Procedures to get assistance
  Repair procedures
Procedures of making appointments
Procedures for handling mail

Other items of concern to secretaries are those that also concern other company employees, such as these:

Fringe benefits
Insurance benefits
Vacation time
Sick leave
Maternity leave
Absentee policies
Stock options

In addition, each secretary must determine from his own boss the following:

Whether the boss is to be disturbed (1) if he is on the telephone, and (2) if
  he is in a meeting
Names of people he is always "in" for
Preferred dictation routine
Length of lunch hour and coffee breaks

When you have compiled this information, prepare your own job-description sheet and a secretarial handbook for orientation of new secretaries to your office. A well-prepared handbook will be a daily reference source as well as an orientation device for the new secretary. At a propitious moment, put yourself down for an appointment with your boss and discuss this handbook with him. Perhaps he will have additional ideas to incorporate in either the job description or the handbook, and you will have the opportunity of making a positive contribution to your company and to the secretarial profession. Remember, your boss may not realize that essential information has been omitted, from the secretarial point of view. If you simply blame him, you are closing important communications lines. If you help him, you are opening important communications lines.

You need to learn your job well, because every employee is periodically evaluated. If the evaluation is "Poor," the employee will usually be told what is wrong and what should be done. Several "Poor" evaluations may cause termination of employment. "Good" evaluations usually result in pay or promotional increases.

Part of the evaluation is on the use of essential skills on the job, but a great portion will be on how the employee functions in relationships with other people and with the boss. Your basic attitude toward your work is also an important factor.

> There were two secretaries in one office who functioned so efficiently that it was unnecessary to supply a vacation replacement. They agreed to take over for each other at vacation time. In their spare moments, they taught each other essentials of their jobs. They learned what matters should be taken care of and what could wait. When secretary A went on vacation, secretary B spent only ten or fifteen minutes at a time, as she could spare it from her own work, at the desk of secretary A. Her boss was never at a disadvantage, and the necessary work of boss A was done. At the close of the day, both secretarial desks were clean and orderly. The further bonus was that secretary A was not unduly overloaded when she returned, and she knew her work had been done properly in her absence.

ASSERT YOUR PERSONALITY

As you work toward building a personal relationship with your boss, and before the relationship becomes set, deliberately provoke a situation. Do something to test the wind — see what it takes to get to the boss. Face up to the fact that you are entering into a personal relationship and enjoy it. You can put off the building of a relationship for years, but if you do, you will be mediocre. Face up to the situation during your first days on the job — carry the ball. Take the initiative and make it easy for the boss to talk to you. Help him teach you your job. Don't be the shrinking violet, be the dynamic, aromatic rose.

Suggested Projects

Select a panel of four class members to play another "Game-Game Show." Your professor has all the materials to determine "How Good Are Your Human Relations?"

Select three or four college administrators and invite them to a role-playing game. Select three or four students to play the role of secretary to each of the administrators. Ask each administrator to think up a situation that will cause each secretary to react to a human-relations problem. After the game is completed, ask the administrators to rank 1-2-3-4 the secretaries' reactions and to explain the reasons for the rankings.

7

Develop
Good
Work Habits

If your current work habits are anything like your habits of dressing, how do you classify them? Look at your dressing area, your dresser drawers, and your room. Are you organized? Do you have a regular routine?

Do you frequently keep others waiting while you finish dressing? Do you find it difficult to get to work on time each morning? Do you find it necessary to comb your hair or adjust your clothing after arriving at school or work?

Good work habits are absolutely essential to the successful completion of a good day's work. If you want to be successful, start now to develop habits of efficiency.

Start with something you know well – the way you organize your time getting ready for work. Arrange your dressing area and set goals to meet. Time yourself by your usual pattern of getting dressed. How many minutes do you spend now in getting ready to face your day?

ORGANIZE YOURSELF

Sit down now and list, step by step, what you did this morning getting dressed, following a pattern similar to the following:

Activity	M	T	W	T	F	S	S
Shut off the alarm							
Fumble for robe and slippers							
Exercise							
Wash face, hands							
Fix breakfast and eat							
Shower and brush teeth							
Comb hair							
Apply makeup – or shave							
Dress							

Your list may not be precisely the same, but it should be similar. As you go through these procedures each morning, notice particularly whether you follow a pattern closely or whether you deviate, indicating that you do not have a habitual sequence for dressing. Write down the amount of time it takes you to go through each step of your routine.

Now you should consider what you can do to shorten the time it takes you – to establish and follow a new, more efficient pattern of getting dressed. How can you arrange your materials so that you can dress in a minimum amount of time without sacrificing quality? In the business world, this is called an efficiency study or a time-and-motion study, and *it is necessary to make a written record* of each step in the process if you are to increase your efficiency.

Although you may feel a little silly making your first written record of getting dressed, you may be surprised to discover after a few days of effort how much time you actually waste, when you can produce the same results in less time. Each step in the process of increasing your efficiency must be examined – none can be skipped – so make that written record today!

When you have the record written down, study it carefully for ways to reorganize your time and your dressing area so that you can get the same job accomplished in less time. Keep this record and work on this particular job for a two-week period. Save each day's records, and at the end of the two weeks, compare your first listing with the final listing. If you have really worked at organizing yourself, you should have achieved a good saving of time.

Through the trial period of your efficiency study on habits of getting dressed, you should learn quite a bit about yourself, if you will view yourself objectively. Now you should start to apply these same techniques to organizing yourself in the classroom and office situation. Just as you did with your dressing area, you must begin by organizing your work area.

ORGANIZE YOUR WORK AREA

At the beginning of this chapter, you were asked to take a critical look at your work area. Take another critical look now – is there any difference? Examine the work area in Figure 7-1 – is the secretary organized? On what did you base your conclusion? The

FIGURE 7-1

items you use for your work in this classroom should be on your desk in an organized fashion. When your professor wants you to take notes, your pen and pad must be ready for instant response or you will be wasting valuable time — the professor's and yours. Are you guilty of holding up the work of the entire class because you must search for that elusive pen? You know what you may need in this classroom — have these items on your desk whether you use them every day or not.

Having determined the needs of your job, you must study your motions in utilizing these materials. How could the desk in Figure 7-1 be made more efficient? Are you constantly shifting things around on your desk as you move from one task to another? If so, you are wasting time. How can you organize your desk to eliminate shifting as much as possible? How many times have you gone on a fishing expedition for that typing eraser that has rolled under the typewriter? Where can you put the eraser so that it is always ready and available?

You are the secretary in Figure 7-1. Suppose you are interrupted in a typing chore to answer the telephone — where do you keep your message pad? Suppose your pen fails to write as you take a message — do you have to fumble for another pen or pencil, or even embarrass yourself by asking the caller to wait while you find something to write with?

A little thought given to these kinds of activities will greatly increase your organization and thus your efficiency. Good habits of efficiency will prepare you for gaining good work habits concerning major areas of your job.

ACCEPT RESPONSIBILITY

Responsibility was discussed in Chapter 1 as related to personality and working with others, in Chapter 3 as related to developing a personal dress code, in Chapter 4 as related to becoming a member of the office team, and in Chapter 6 as related to building relationships with the boss. The secretary also accepts the responsibility of developing work habits that will allow the strengthening of other responsibilities.

One of the best habits you can form is to *listen* effectively. Listen to instructions — carefully. Every instruction given to you is important, no matter how short it may be. Listen — then record. Probably the largest single reason for student failure is to ask clarifying questions. If you find it difficult to ask questions, start with tiny ones. Learn to ask small questions easily — then just keep right on asking until you understand exactly what you are supposed to do.

Many workers — and students — assume that they will be able to find answers to their questions elsewhere. This simply is not true. No one knows what your professor or boss wants except your professor or your boss — so stop assuming and start asking. Asking questions is an art in itself, so let's explore several ways of asking those small but so important questions.

One of the cardinal sins of asking questions is to interrupt the boss before he has finished giving all the instructions. When this happens, it is an indication that you are not listening effectively. Therefore, timing your question is most important. If your boss shows irritation when you ask a question, take this as a clue that your timing is poor.

Assuming that your timing is right, then start asking your questions very simply — don't make a federal case of it. For example, suppose your instructions are as follows:

> Take a memo to Mr. Brown — and it is important that he gets this within the next hour, so do a rush job. Oh, and send a copy to Bob. I'll be in the sales meeting for the next two hours.

How many questions do you need to ask? Remember, playing assumptions is a dangerous game. You should ask first, "Is that *Larry* Brown or *Jack* Brown?" If you wait until your boss has left for that meeting to discover that you don't know *which* Mr. Brown, you are going to be in an awkward position. Now you need to know whether to initial the memo with his initials, or to indicate his signature with your initials in parentheses, or just how to put that personal touch of a signature to the memo. How would you ask that question? Well, you might ask, "How would you like the signature handled?"

Your instructions were to do a rush job because it is important that Mr. Brown gets the memo within the hour. How is it going to get there? Are you to personally carry it? Are you to send it by courier? Would you send it through the regular channels of mail? Don't assume — how does the boss want the job done? How will you ask this question? Perhaps you could say something like, "Shall I hand-carry the memo to Mr. Brown?"

Still another question is needed for understanding of instructions. Can you identify it? Yes — "Bob *Green*, Bob *Long*, or Bob *Smith*?" Sometimes common names are too common for comfort in an office, and you must be sure you have the right name or you can create all sorts of uncomfortable situations.

There is still one last question you should ask. Did you clarify *where* the sales meeting is to be held?

You can see from this example that even three short sentences by your boss may need considerable clarification. Short, simple, direct questions are best. Not only does it clarify the situation for you, it relieves the boss of the responsibility of trying to ensure that he has thought of absolutely everything you need to know. He can answer your questions and still be organizing his mind for the sales meeting coming up. He can have a free mind because he knows that you got all the answers you needed before he left. By relieving your boss of this responsibility and accepting it for yourself, you will be displaying maturity — not, as so many inexperienced people believe, ignorance. It takes a mature person to realize that the boss's mind is really elsewhere, that he is taking care of a necessary piece of correspondence as quickly as possible and relying on you to take care of the details. Part of your responsibility is, therefore, to ask questions, recording the instructions so that you can take care of the details properly.

Your boss may sometimes give you so many instructions at one time that you wonder how he can think that fast. To be ready for any set of instructions, make it a habit to write down *all* instructions, no matter how short they may be. Suppose that in the last example, you did not jot down which Mr. Brown your boss said should get the memo. You *thought* you would remember that. Now, as soon as you get back to your own desk after getting Mr. Vancil off to his meeting, your phone rings and there is a short conversation. When you hang up, you look at your notes and — "Oh, no! *Which* Mr. Brown did he say?"

> Suppose you answer the telephone and find the boss's wife wants to talk to her husband as soon as he is free from the sales meeting. You start to record the message, but you are interrupted by another secretary who needs assistance. You think you will remember the message, so you don't complete it. You spend a few minutes with the secretary and resume your work. Mr. Vancil returns from the sales meeting, goes to lunch, returns to the office, and at 3:00 P.M. it suddenly occurs to you that you promised to tell him Mrs. Vancil called. . . .

There is just no substitute for the written word!

The more organized you become, the better work habits you develop, the more responsibility you are ready to accept. The more responsibility you accept successfully, the greater your value to the boss and to the organization for which you work.

HANDLING CONFIDENTIAL MATERIALS

In the development of good work habits, there are many tricks of the trade you can learn. One of the best examples of this can be illustrated in discussing the handling of confidential materials. You will remember that Chapter 6 contained information about the trust that the boss must have in his secretary. It is the responsibility of the secretary to make sure that this trust is not misplaced. It is most important that the boss be able to discuss anything and everything with his secretary, that the secretary can be trusted to handle any type of confidential material. A loose tongue, a careless remark, can create serious problems.

> Consider the secretary who told another secretary "confidentially" that he had overheard a remark that one of the men in the department was going to be asked to resign, only to discover before the afternoon was over that the rumor had not only reached the man involved, the man had reached the secretary's desk and demanded to see his boss.

A serious situation can result from such a mistake. The man involved is left with no way to save face and is subjected to the remarks or questioning looks of other members of the department. The boss is placed in an awkward position of having to apologize for the rumor's getting out — and of course, he knows who was responsible, which causes him to seriously question the integrity and ability of the secretary. What other ramifications can you identify that could result from this one careless remark?

How can you keep prying eyes away from the material that you are typing? Sometimes the location of your desk can be an important factor. There are times, however, when anyone standing by your desk can easily see whatever is in the typewriter. Again, organization of your work area is important — you should have cover sheets available to place over finished pages that you place in order on your desk. If you make a habit of always using cover sheets (or folders) for everything you type, then there will be no indication to others in the office that this particular material is confidential.

> One secretary who was unfamiliar with most tricks of the trade, following instructions that a certain employee should not be allowed to see what was being typed, was so flustered when she discovered that that person was approaching her desk that she actually grabbed the typewriter cover and jammed it down on the typewriter!

Can you imagine the look on the face of the person approaching — not to mention the concern and curiosity immediately aroused by the secretary's actions? A secretary can certainly find better ways of handling such situations. What would you have done?

Depending on the location of your typewriter and the location of the person at your desk, there are many tricks that you might use to block the material from view. The easiest device to use is the "arm block" — simply rest your arms casually on the typewriter with your hands carefully draped across the finished portion of the paper (see Figure 7-2). Another body block may be the sideways "elbow on the machine" trick (see Figure 7-3). If nothing else comes to mind, you might simply and casually remove the paper from the machine and tuck it into the folder or under the cover sheet as if you had completed that page. Such actions need not interfere in the slightest with the conversation with the person at your desk. Handling confidential material does require alertness to the presence of others and the assumption of a casual exterior when you are involved in this type of work.

It is a wise secretary who occasionally checks to see if the work left on the desk is rearranged during a necessary absence from the

The Arm Block

The Body Block

FIGURE 7-2

FIGURE 7-3

desk. If you are working with confidential material, never leave your desk without first securing the material — putting it away — so that it cannot easily be read in your absence. Human nature includes a great deal of curiosity, so when you do leave your desk, occasionally place a ruler, or a small piece of paper, at an angle against an identifying mark that only you will recognize. When you return to your desk, check the position of the marker. If it is not as you left it, then you need to become more watchful and more careful in your handling of material.

There are many other tricks to handling material in the office. As you gain experience, you will expand your knowledge of these techniques by adapting those used by other secretaries. Even now you should start to watch for these techniques as you visit various business offices. Some you will develop on your own, and they will suit better than any other. Good work habits make it possible to develop better techniques, because you are constantly seeking ways to increase your efficiency in the office.

HANDLING TECHNICAL MATERIAL

There are many kinds of secretarial positions, as was pointed out at the very beginning of this book. Many of them are technical in nature, with terminology peculiarly their own — law, medicine, and education, to mention but three.

One technical area that seems to permeate the entire field, however, is that of data processing. It is not necessary for a secretary to be well versed in legal, medical, or educational terminology; but it is becoming increasingly necessary for him to have some acquaintance with data-processing terminology.

Data processing is a term that has an elusive and mysterious quality. What is this term that you hear so often? What is there about it that makes you a little leery of talking about it — or even listening to others talk about it?

Well, this term is relatively new in the business world, and it really has a terminology all its own. The terminology is what gives it that elusive and mysterious quality, because of unfamiliarity with the words. Most of them are very easy to understand — once you have an explanation of them in words you are familiar with.

Data processing is simply — to turn it around — the processing of data. The business world has processed data since the first account was kept. Secretaries process data every day — you move things around, and you obtain various results with that material. For example, bookkeepers and accountants manually record sales, invoices of goods received, the amount of profit or loss on the merchandise, and other such information. From these figures, they are able to produce certain reports that will show the entire picture of purchases and sales over a certain period of time. They have processed their data. A machine cannot handle English, so any work assigned to the machine must be translated into numbers — machine language. Thus, the work that the bookkeepers or accountants formerly did by hand is now put into machine language, and entered into a machine that has been programmed (told what to do) to turn out the same results much faster and more accurately. This kind of machine production, replacing manual production, is called electronic data processing — or simply data processing.

The area of data processing has increased so rapidly that even businessmen have difficulty in keeping up with the capabilities of the machines as new and better ways are devised for handling data. The people who work in the data-processing area have adapted the English language to suit their needs and have evolved an entire language of their own. Thus, when they speak to people not in data processing and not familiar with the language, they sound almost as if they are speaking a foreign tongue. This can sound impressive — but remember, it can hide an abundance of ignorance, too. Pick up a few words in a foreign tongue if you want to impress people with your intellectual ability. Pick up a few terms in data processing if you want to sound like an expert. You don't even have to understand them very well to be impressive to those not versed in the terminology. The pseudoexpert will, however, be unable to impress the real experts in the field.

There is so much to learn about data processing — what should the secretary know about it? A secretary should know generally what is accomplished through the use of data processing, and should know enough to know when to gain more knowledge in the area. When a job involves data processing to a great extent, then the secretary should certainly start to learn about the subject. Every secretary in today's business world should have an introductory course in data processing, to become acquainted with its basic terminology, its background and history, and its functions, and to obtain an insight into the business of data processing.

A *Glossary of Data Processing Terms* is available from the U.S. Government Printing Office in Washington, D.C. It never hurts to have such a glossary on your desk, and it will be invaluable to you as you work in any office. When you hear terms not contained in this glossary, do not hesitate to add them to it. As a secretary, you will find that the best dictionary is the one you yourself construct of the words heard over and over in the office. When you order your glossary, ask about the availability of other types of glossaries, because what is said here about data processing is true of other technical fields, such as law, medicine, engineering, or construction.

It is interesting and challenging to study the technical glossaries. It is helpful to construct shorthand outlines beside each word — consulting shorthand books, professors of shorthand, or other secretaries when outlines give difficulty. Increased efficiency comes from the study of these outlines as they become part of your basic vocabulary.

No one expects the secretary to know about programming or systems analysis — but they do expect a secretary to be able to take dictation, which means that there must be a command of the technical terminology involved in the day-to-day correspondence of an office. When you feel as though you are on an island of ignorance, watching the ship Intellect slip past in the dark, then it is your responsibility to ask questions. Ask for explanations!

As you obtain explanations, ask also for reasons. Write down *why* a certain procedure is followed. It is not enough to follow procedure by rote, a secretary needs to understand the job — and *why* is one of the most important questions to be asked. Do not rely on memory; memory will fail you just when you need it most. *Keep procedures written down.* When you have recorded a number of procedures, sort and classify them. Prepare a secretarial handbook of company data-processing procedures, and update it periodically.

A new employee will find it helpful to make a friend of one of the secretaries who has been with the firm for an extended period of time and who is successful on the job. This secretary will become a fountain of wisdom, making it possible to learn the job much more quickly than would otherwise be possible.

Knowledge and understanding take the mystery away from a new procedure. When new data-processing equipment — or any other, for that matter — comes into the office, be willing to learn about it. It may not be necessary to become an expert operator, but learning its basic operation will provide the background for you to be ready for its use. It will give you some understanding of its function as it relates to your particular job.

As the secretary, you are responsible for interpreting total meaning to the reader of correspondence — routine or technical — prepared by your office. As you accept this responsibility, instead of assuming that the reader knows what you are talking about, assume he does not know. It takes a knowledgeable person to make a correct interpretation to the layman not versed in the technical jargon of data processing.

Remember, your boss knows the terminology so well that he will not even consider your needs; he just automatically assumes that you know what he is talking about. It is your responsibility to stop him during dictation to ask for clarification or information or instructions. Unless you ask, the boss assumes you know. He doesn't use a crystal ball — and besides, he doesn't have time to waste in continually asking if you understand. Each person has certain responsibilities inherent in his job with the company, and yours cannot be shifted to another person. You must take time to communicate.

No matter what instructions or details a boss gives, the secretary will be safe with a notebook close at hand to *write it down*! If it is unique and new, notes should be saved. If it concerns procedure, it should be added to the written procedures. Never rely on memory. If it is definitive, add it to the terminology collection and form a shorthand outline to go with it.

In sticky situations, the written word is invaluable.

A secretary sometimes takes dictation from as many as ten or fifteen different people. A secretary may be assigned to one person, but have a multiple responsibility for correspondence. In this circumstance, it becomes increasingly important to write down everything — for the secretary's work must be pleasing to each individual. Total flexibility is necessary when working under these conditions, and that flexibility is the secretary's responsibility. This type of work is exciting because of exposure to constantly changing ideas, availability to a contrast in viewpoints, and the opportunity to learn various ways of doing the same job. A secretary will be more successful in completing correspondence by taking an interest in what is written. If you think about the message being conveyed, you will not hesitate to change a sentence to make the meaning more clear. All changes, however, should be double-checked with the writer.

SELECTING NEW OFFICE EQUIPMENT

As you become more efficient as a secretary, you will be searching for office equipment that will make your job easier and that will make it possible to increase efficiency. You will be more aware of your needs than will anyone else; therefore, before you ask your employer to buy additional equipment, you should explore the market to find what equipment is available that will do the best job. Short visits to various office-equipment companies will reveal new styles, designs, and colors that are available. You can also be aware of new types of supplies on the market to make the job of the secretary easier and more pleasant.

Explore the various kinds of filing cabinets, for example. They come in many styles and colors. They use various styles and sizes of folders. The materials used in new equipment are very different from those used only a few years ago. You should try to keep up with the latest in office equipment, so that you are prepared to advise your boss on either equipment that you need, or equipment he suggests. Check current magazines on office equipment and supplies in the periodicals section of the library. Obtain brochures of equipment and keep them readily accessible in a file. You can obtain prices from office-supply houses if they are not included in the brochures.

As you go from office to office, be inquisitive about types of equipment. Make notes on what you discover. Gathering such data can fill certain time gaps when your work seems to be slow. Do you know what "office landscaping" means? Study your classroom or office. What changes could you make in the arrangement to create a more efficient and pleasant working area? Would you need to add anything? How would you justify the need for the addition?

SLACK-TIME PROJECTS

There are times when you are caught up with the normal work and there is nothing that really needs attention. Good work habits decree, however, that a secretary always appear to be busy. Projects, such as building an equipment file, can receive your attention during slack times. Have you explored the lateral files? Do you need to explore microfilm filing? What kinds of new storage cabinets are available? Can you justify a new purchase? How long has it been since you cleaned the files? Why should a new filing cabinet be ordered, when there are so many folders in your present cabinet that might be eliminated or reduced to microfilm? How long should files be maintained before disposing of the information? Remember the filing rules about this? Consult your employer about special kinds of files that may require special consideration. It must be reemphasized, however, that the files are your primary responsibility, and you must make decisions about which should be transferred to an inactive file and which can be completely eliminated. If this is done fairly often, the job will never consume too much of your time, and you will always have a current set of files, well organized for efficient use.

Many secretaries are afraid to throw things away. File cabinets are stuffed with files that are used only a few times. A look into some of the cabinets will reveal drawers so packed that it seems impossible to put in one more folder. A closer inspection would show that at least one-fourth of the files in each drawer could probably be thrown away completely. A secretary who is efficient would take the challenge to build the best set of files in the company. This is one of the tasks in which a secretary can really take pride — the filing cabinet is the best place in the world to find the history of the firm in which you work. A study of the files shows style of correspondence and kinds of activities to be expected on the job; and, further, the files reflect the true picture of the business operation of the office. A secretary who maintains an efficient set of files can very justly take great pride in this job.

PRIDE IN WORK

The development of good work habits will result in pride in a job well done. Are you proud of your work habits today? If you can say "Yes," you are an exception. You can and should take pride in the things you do well, and you should recognize your own strengths in this area, but never be completely satisfied, because there is always room for improvement. You should find a certain pride in always being prepared, in having your materials properly arranged for the most efficient use, and in the appearance of your work and your work area.

According to the efficiency experts, there is a divided opinion about whether the appearance of a working area is really indicative of efficiency. In the eyes of the public visiting the office, however, the appearance of the secretary's work area is certainly an important factor in judging the office. The first impression is still of prime importance, and the secretary's area plays as important a role in this impression as the appearance of his work plays in presenting his boss to the outside world. Taking pride in your work becomes more important as you consider the implications of your actions on the image of your boss and the firm for which you work. The secretarial job, like every other job in the firm, is an important one in the total production of the company. When this fact is understood, pride in a job well done has more meaning to a person, and promotes motivation in acquiring new skills.

Suggested Projects

Ask four or five secretaries to serve as a panel to discuss "Secretarial Efficiency." Set aside 15–20 minutes of the time period for a contest: The class will work on their various tasks and the panel members will observe. At the completion of the time period, ask the panel members to name a "Miss Efficiency."

Invite a local efficiency expert from a business firm to talk to the class. Use the expertise you've gained from issuing prior invitations of this nature.

Your company has hired an efficiency expert to evaluate all clerical areas within the company. The purpose is to determine the following:

A. Are additional typists, stenographers, and secretaries really needed?

B. Should a central filing system be established?

C. Should training programs in clerical skills be offered by the company?

D. Should selected employees be encouraged to upgrade their skills at the local college?

You want to make a good impression on the efficiency expert, and you expect him to be on the job today, so watch your work area as you tackle your daily tasks.

You are the secretary for the Business Division at your college. Your employer (your professor) has told you that you will be moving to a new office. You are given the floor plan in Figure 7-4. Your boss has told you

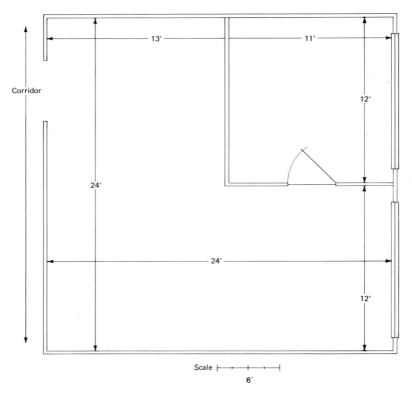

FIGURE 7-4

to plan the layout and suggest equipment and any new types of supplies that will be necessary (you have no equipment or furniture to consider at present). He has not limited your budget at this time, but you know you will need to justify your requests. Plan for a desired result, but also plan for a minimum selection. Submit your written suggestions and attach samples (brochures) and cost figures. You have three typists in your area,

and the space must provide for three professors as well. Remember —
professors need a little privacy. Measure your professor's desk, stenographers' desks, file cabinets, etc., to determine size and space needed. Be
sure to leave "moving" room. Plan at least one bookcase and one file
cabinet for each professor.

8

The Art
of Dictation

Many secretaries dictate letters. In both large and small companies, the secretary can take the responsibility for the more routine letters in order to relieve the boss for more important tasks. In many instances, an employer may brief the secretary on the nature or tone of the correspondence. The secretary takes notes and, in turn, prepares or dictates the actual letter.

For example, the boss may say:

> Miss Brown, please answer this letter to Dick Rogers — tell him I appreciated hearing from him, that I wish I could accommodate his request, but that I have a meeting in Chicago that week. Ask him for a rain check. Then write to Frances Bacon and tell her I received the package of materials and will take prompt action on distribution. Write a memo to Jack Jones and ask him to submit any names of persons he may recommend for that opening that was announced in Purchasing yesterday.

The secretary will then return to her office and actually compose the letters on the typewriter or dictate them to a stenographer or to a dictation machine. For this reason, a professional secretary should study dictation techniques.

Obviously, the secretary must have a good background in business English and business letter writing to be successful in dictating good-to-excellent letters. This statement is, of course, not limited to the secretary — anyone who dictates a letter must have such a background in order to obtain the communication desired.

"Why? Surely I can dictate a letter." Of course you can! To be completely honest, anyone can dictate correspondence just as anyone can breathe. The real question is, How good is your dictation? Professional athletes undoubtedly breathe more effectively and efficiently than does the ordinary citizen. The professional business correspondent undoubtedly dictates more effectively and efficiently than does the ordinary citizen. Anyone can train himself to do a better job of either.

Furthermore, just as the athlete who gets lax about his exercise gets out of shape, the dictator who gets lax about his dictating practice gets out of shape. Ask any businessman if he can dictate a good business letter, and you will probably get one of two responses: (1) Ego will evoke a positive answer. Many executives can indeed dictate a good business letter. (2) Insecurity will evoke a somewhat wishy-washy answer, usually ending with a statement like, "I prefer to write my correspondence or reports in longhand so that I can proofread them and be sure they are correct." Many executives realize certain personal shortcomings in dictation, but find it difficult to admit such frailty. A further look at dictating skills would ease the minds of these executives. Most executives do, indeed, need some assistance in developing better dictation techniques – just as the secretary consistently needs to be on the alert for better ways of preparing finished copy.

Write a report in longhand – what a waste of time! Ordinarily, rates of dictation will average 80-100 words per minute, as opposed to an average longhand rate of 10-30 words a minute – a difference of approximately 70 words per minute. The use of dictation would take less than half the time of writing a piece of correspondence in longhand. In addition to the time factor, if a machine is used to dictate a report, the first tape can be handed to the secretary, who can prepare the required rough draft of it while the executive works on the second tape. Thus, by the time the report is completed, the first pages are on the desk of the executive, ready to be reworked. Office production is thereby accelerated.

If the executive is dictating directly to the secretary, the time saved is still significant, and while the secretary prepares the rough draft of the report, the executive is free to work on other material.

Most executive-secretary teams have a good working relationship; but there are few secretaries who will not admit that the boss could use some help in dictating techniques. A periodic self-examination of dictating techniques or an occasional self-administered brush-up course will result in better dictating habits.

The dictator who periodically reviews his dictating techniques will increase not only his own effectiveness, but also the efficiency of his secretary. These increases are measurable in dollars and cents.

A large company, like an individual, has a personality so far as the public is concerned. Whether a company will endure and prosper may depend upon the kind of face it presents to the public. Its personality is created in several ways — through advertising, through services, and through personal relationships and correspondence; but after that initial contact, many people know the company only through letters. They form an opinion of the individual or the company from the letters they receive.

WRITING EFFECTIVELY

Effective business writing is clear and forceful. To achieve this effect, the writer must use short words. In order to allow the reader time to digest what you have said, express only one idea in each sentence, thereby creating the desire to act. To enforce this desire, use active verbs. Capture reader interest with the first sentence, then keep your action moving to hold reader interest to the end of the letter.

Each letter is a challenge to the writer, but the most challenging to write is, perhaps, the negative one. People do not like to cause unhappiness, frustration, or ill will, but it is sometimes necessary to say no. In giving a negative response, you need not be too blunt; it isn't necessary to raise welts on the reader. Use care that you do not take your frustration, at having to say no, out on him. Approach your task with concern and confidence.

Explain the reason for the rejection. If the reason is confidential, at least assure the reader that his request was thoroughly considered. You should be sparing with apologies or you may sound insincere. Any alternative should be offered at the beginning of the letter, letting the refusal come at the end. When you can write a negative letter in a positive tone, you will have acquired and mastered the technique of letter writing.

It is a common practice for executives to refer certain letters to the secretary for reply, even though the letters have been addressed to them personally. When a letter is referred to you for an answer, it is important to stress that the person addressed was concerned that the reader receive the most accurate information possible and, therefore, referred the letter to you. Your reader should be given the impression that *you* are the person best qualified to answer him, never that he is being "passed around."

Sometimes the letter is referred to you for you to prepare a response for the signature of the person to whom the letter was

138

addressed. In this instance, you should strive to use the writing style of the other person.

If your letter is a long one, use the last paragraph to sum up the main points in it. If you want your reader to do something, put your request in the closing sentence. It is the impact of this sentence that lingers in the mind of the reader.

THE QUIET SECRETARY

The easiest way to study dictation techniques is through the use of a machine. There are numerous dictation machines on the market, but all are similar. If you lack access to a dictation machine, the use of a tape recorder will allow you to practice dictating techniques, with the exception that you will not have the practice with the index strip, which is an instruction slip for the secretary.

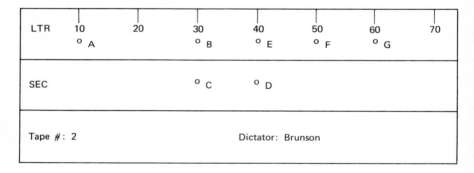

A-B = length of first letter

C-D = shows secretary that a correction or special instruction is on the tape between these two points. The secretary would listen to C-D before starting at A.

E-F = length of second letter

F-G = length of third letter

Tape # = numbered in sequence for convenience of the secretary

Dictator = name of dictator eliminates any confusion that might arise, especially when the secretary types for several dictators.

FIGURE 8-1

The best way to improve your speaking ability is to listen to yourself — listen with certain objectives in mind. Learn to use the machine efficiently, and your dictating tasks will become much easier and more natural. Your machine should be set up with magnetic tape and index strip in place. An index strip (see Figure 8-1) is used to record the length of letters and to indicate where the secretary will find particular instructions. The index strip is essential to the efficient transcription of letters by the secretary. When the strip is used efficiently, the secretary will find it unnecessary to type a rough draft of any correspondence. He can correctly place the letter and produce an error-free piece of correspondence.

The microphone (Figure 8-2) will contain a speaker's button, an instruction button, and a length-of-letter button. The use of these buttons is essential to effective dictation. Error-free dictation is possible because you will be able to back up and redictate at any particular point.

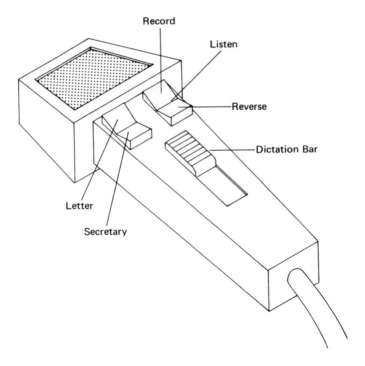

FIGURE 8-2

Suppose you have dictated a letter and suddenly realize that you will need to add a paragraph or a sentence near the beginning of the letter. By pressing the instruction button, you immediately alert the secretary to the fact that there is a special instruction on this tape and that this instruction should be picked up before typing the material. You can now proceed with the instruction on where you want this paragraph or sentence inserted, dictate the material, and mark the end of the special instruction by touching the instruction button again.

It is most important to master the proper technique of using the microphone. Most mikes are so sensitive that even a whisper will be transmitted quite audibly. Too many secretaries suffer through hurricanes because the dictator blows smoke into the mike. The mike should be held *at an angle*, so that the sound travels *over* it, not into it. It should be held further away from the mouth than is the telephone receiver — a good deal further away.

It will take practice to make the planning for dictation a routine consideration in letter-writing skill. As this practice is developing your skill, you must consider other factors that will contribute to your ability to communicate through letters.

UNDERSTANDING REACTIONS TO WORDS

Business English and business letter writing stress the fact that the emotions of the reader affect the effectiveness of the communication. Words are used to express ideas — ideas to be interpreted by the reader.

Why do certain words have one effect on one person and another effect on another person? That this is so probably lies in the fact that each person associates words in terms of his own background and experience. Try this experiment, comparing your responses with those of your friends, and you may see the connotative power of words on different people. Using the following list of words, place a circle around those you like more than you dislike, and draw a line through those you dislike more than you like. Respond in terms of your *first* — emotional — reaction.

efficient	*wisdom*	*challenge*
portrait	*prejudice*	*advice*

antagonize	*liberation*	*train*
possession	*peace*	*shorthand*
advantage	*home*	*routine*
beating	*loving*	*exciting*
plus	*minus*	

As you compare results with other persons, you may discover that some of the words brought entirely different mental images to each of you. For example, *train* might have meant a "locomotive" to one, and "to condition" to another.

When someone reads a letter, his first reaction to the words is on an emotional level. If you know the person you are writing to, you can use words that will be acceptable to him and avoid those that would antagonize him. If you know the response you want to obtain from your reader, you can select those words that will cause a favorable reaction. After a letter has been written, it should be proofread from the reader's point of view. Do not sign it until you feel the words used will elicit the desired response.

PLANNING FOR DICTATION

To avoid the waste of productive time, the letters to be written should be planned before the secretary is called into the office or before the use of the dictation machine. To be most effective, the writer should plan the approach to the specific letter. If he knows the reader personally, such planning becomes easier.

The basis for any good letter is the outline. The outline is devised, of course, based upon all the facts. The writer must be familiar with any background correspondence. After the outline has been prepared, visualize your reader sitting across the desk from you, and dictate the letter to him. By letting your own personality come through, your letter will have both individuality and vitality.

There are many things a dictator can do to help the secretary do a better job. The following list should be mastered as a dictation routine:

Organize your thoughts. Know what you are going to say.
Have all necessary reference material (files, statements, letters, sales slips) on your desk.

Enunciate clearly.
If you are interrupted during dictation, stop the machine.
Give the style of correspondence – letter, memo, report.
State the number of carbons to be prepared, before *dictating.*
If a job is rush *– say so!*
Indicate all paragraphs and unusual punctuation marks.
Spell technical words or proper names if they are unusual.
Indicate capitalization before *you say the word to be capitalized.*

Whether you dictate to a real live secretary or the table model, there are certain mannerisms that are distracting:

Coughing, clearing the throat
Talking with cigar, cigarette, or pipe in mouth
Rattling papers
Eating
Chewing gum
Pacing while talking
Fumbling with the microphone
Holding your hand over your mouth
Holding the microphone too far away
Holding the microphone too close
Talking before pressing the dictate bar – or after releasing it
Slurring syllables or word endings

You must remember that a secretary is not a mind reader. As you begin to dictate, there are certain instructions to be given for each piece of correspondence:

Type of correspondence – letter, memo, report
Number of carbon copies
Name and address of the addressee
Attention line and/or subject line
Letter form (if varying from normal procedure)
Recipients of carbons

After the letter has been typed, read it carefully before you sign it. Check it to be sure that each phrase is concise and clear – that the tone of the letter is positive, friendly, and reasonably sure to elicit the desired response.

CRITIQUING YOUR LETTERS

To increase effectiveness as a letter writer, critique your own work. Is it written with a clear idea of what you want the reader to do? Is each fact correctly stated? Did you arrange your letter in the most logical sequence? Did you establish rapport with the reader by beginning the letter with something that interests him? Did you mentally seat the reader across the desk while you were dictating, so that you could check the effect of your words? Is the letter conversational — friendly?

Did you avoid trying to be impressive with the use of large words? Remember — short words help to give clearness to a sentence. Check the length of sentences; long, complex sentences are difficult to read for accurate meaning. Sometimes sentences become complex enough to serve as a noose for the writer, and sometimes we unintentionally give the reader a good laugh at our own expense. A sentence written to convey one thought may convey quite another. For example, let's analyze the following sentences. What do they *say* and what do they *intend to say*?

1. We have just received the information that your jewelry display was robbed by our salesman. [Did the salesman do it? Did he report it? What was he doing with it?]

2. I shall await your check in the enclosed envelope. [Be careful that you don't smother.]

3. The "Softie" is such a comfortable shoe that most women wear nothing else. [Would you use the sentence in an ad?]

4. This will acknowledge receipt of the letter referring to the defective water pump, which was placed in our files. [Besides being bulky, won't it get the files dirty?]

5. Being reduced, you will understand our position on refunds. [Are you for sale? Did you lose weight?]

Analyze each of your own sentences carefully to avoid misunderstanding. Be sure you said what you meant to say.

What about the use of technical terms — will your reader understand? Do you need to clarify any term you have used?

Check your letter format, punctuation, and spelling. Careless errors indicate a tendency toward careless thinking. You may rely heavily on your typist for these chores — but only the writer of the letter is responsible, in the final analysis, for the letter in its entirety.

When you first begin to dictate letters, your progress will seem slow. Dictation is an art, and like any other form of art, it takes time to perfect. For the professional secretary, dictation is an art well worth developing as a skill for future professional growth.

Suggested Projects

Ask five executives if they dictate all their material or if they use longhand for some of the letters and reports. Find out how many of them use a dictation machine and how many use both a secretary and a machine. Find out how many executives have been provided with a machine but do not use it. Write down your findings and promote a classroom discussion on your answers.

Use the following letters for dictation practice. Instructions for machine use are in brackets. Instructions to the secretary are underscored and should be dictated. Check your machine for tape and index strip. When these are in place, push the letter button, then put the dictate bar into "record" position.

This is a letter. Make two extra carbon copies. Send this letter to Professor Oldman W. Black, Accounting Department, Northern Virginia Community College, Alexandria, Virginia 22311. Dear Professor Black: Subject: CPA Seminar, January 12-14, 19—. We wish to thank you for the very interesting discussion you led at our recent CPA Seminar; you alerted us to situations that might develop within our area as new changes in legislation are initiated; and you stimulated our thoughts so that we would take positive action. Send one carbon to Tom Jones, our president, and one to L. E. Smith, same address as Prof. Black. Smith is the head of the department. [Release dictate bar, press letter button to mark end of letter.]

Now listen to the letter you have just dictated, carefully checking against the suggestions in your textbook. If your secretary is expert in the use of punctuation, you might dictate only unusual punctuation and let him handle the rest.

Dictating the following letters will help to introduce you to error-free dictation practices. Check your machine to be sure the tape and index strip are in place, and then dictate the following letter:

This is a letter on company letterhead, three copies, to Mr. Thomas P. Lang, President, Lang Electronics, 9201 Glenn Forest Drive, Falls Church, Virginia. Dear Mr. Lang: Enclosed is the engineering-products catalogue you requested in our conversation at lunch today. The model C-940 is described on page 22. Paragraph   Let us know if there is any way we can help you. Yours very truly, [Release dictate bar; flick "review" switch *three* times (*30 words*), listen through "page 22," then put the dictate bar into record position and continue.] Paragraph   Your interest in our equipment is appreciated. Please call me if you need additional information. Very truly yours,   Send blind copies to the sales department and public relations department. [Did you indicate the beginning and end of the letter by pushing the letter button to let your secretary know the length of the letter?]

Let's try another:

This is a letter on company letterhead, two copies to Mr. L.E. Johns, 2611 East 14th Street, Washington, D.C. Dear Mr. Johns: [Release dictate bar, depress review switch *twice*, listen through the name "L. R. Johns," put dictate bar into record position, and continue.] Johns Fabrics, 2611 East 14th Street, Washington, D.C. Dear Mr. Johns: Please accept our apologies for the delay in the shipment of your May drapery-fabric order. Our shipping department has assured us that it will be shipped within four days. [Review paragraph, dictate after "fabric order."] Our shipping department has scheduled the delivery of your order for June 5. Send a copy to the shipping department supervisor. [Indicate end of letter by pushing letter button.]

Using a little imagination, prepare and dictate letters using the following instructions:

Please answer this letter from Dick Rogers and tell him I appreciated hearing from him, that I wish I could accommodate his request, but that I have a meeting in Chicago that week. Ask him for a rain check. Then write to Frances Bacon and tell her I received the package of materials and will take prompt action on distribution. Write a memo to Jack Jones and ask him to submit any names of persons he may recommend for that opening in Purchasing that was announced yesterday.

Changing Careers of the Future

One question always arises in the mind of the secretarial student — what does the future hold? This question is two-pronged: What does the future hold in the way of new skills needed, and what does the future hold in the way of new positions?

One of the recurring questions in the business world today is, Is shorthand becoming extinct? Although there are apparently as many people using shorthand as ever, if not more, the question is raised perhaps because of the little dictation boxes appearing on many executive desks. Companies purchase these units hoping the executives will use them; many do, many do not. Some executives, it seems, still prefer to dictate to someone — to see a human reaction to their work.

NEW SKILLS

Some secretarial positions do not require shorthand as a requisite for the job, but rely solely on the dictation units. The secretaries in these positions are really quite successful, because they do not spend hours in the office taking dictation. The boss can dictate at his desk while the secretary transcribes at *his* desk; thus, more correspondence can be completed in a given time period. These dictation/transcription machines may be particularly advantageous if a secretary is responsible for the correspondence of numerous people. If your training has not included some stress on dictation/ transcription machines, make a conscientious effort to get some practical experience. They look simple to operate, but efficient use requires an acquisition of skill. There are specific techniques to be utilized in the *proper* operation of these units. Learning to operate them takes far less time than does learning to write shorthand. A combination use of shorthand and machine transcription is extremely beneficial in the secretary's position. When an executive has received training in the proper techniques of dictation on these machines, the secretary's use of the transcriber is greatly improved — it is a team effort.

Shorthand machines that record word abbreviations are also popular, particularly in legal offices and in the courtroom. These are operated by secretaries who may never have mastered the skill of shorthand, but have mastered a different skill that can be used in the same profession. Are they any better? Well, that depends, of course, on the degree of skill achieved.

The secretary must also be aware of the new typewriters on the market. Have you had experience on a proportionate-space typewriter? Have you had experience on more than one brand of machine? They are all similar, but models vary, and something new is being added to each new model. Have you had experience with the magnetic-tape Selectric typewriter; the magnetic-card typewriter? the composer? the typewriter with both carbon and fabric ribbon available at the flick of a switch? These kinds of machines are coming into the business world rapidly; the secretary will be challenged to keep abreast of the latest in secretarial-skills equipment, and to become familiar enough with the functioning of such equipment to be able to advise on the feasibility of obtaining it.

There is some work being done on designing a computerized typewriter that will respond to the spoken word. Think what this could mean for reporting conferences, obtaining verbatim recordings such as court trials, or even recording minutes of a board meeting.

This type of new equipment sounds exciting, but perhaps frightening when you think of operating it. Remember, though, if it is designed by man, it can be operated by man. As such innovations spring up in the business world, they bring untold opportunities to the secretary.

When the history of the secretary is recounted, it will reveal that only at the beginning of the twentieth century was the job titled. Think about the changes that have occurred. Although shorthand skill was known at least as early as the time of Moses — when it was called the "winged art" — it took the business world centuries to be ready to make proper use of the skill. Now that the importance and value of secretarial skills are being realized, there is no limit to the exciting opportunities that lie in the future, waiting to be uncovered; therefore, a secretary just entering the business world for the first time must be constantly aware of the needs for changing techniques.

NEW POSITIONS

Consider, for just a moment, the possibility that you will become a secretary to an interplanetary traveler. What changes do you think would be needed to make your job efficient? Could you utilize the same practices and the same equipment that you see in the office today? How would you use an electric typewriter aboard a spaceship? Do you think there will be different kinds of power used for typewriters — or will typing be done by some sort of computer? What would be the effects of computerized letters on the general public and the conservative business community? Well, perhaps the secretarial job in your generation may not reach that drastic a change — yet, who can be sure? Certainly the secretary of tomorrow — *you* — must be aware of the need for flexibility in the use of skills equipment.

On the other hand, has it ever occurred to you that change could just as easily be reversed? The use of electric power is rapidly reaching maximum utilization. Other sources of power must be made available, or better use must be made of the power we now have. Have you ever typed on a manual typewriter? Some secretaries even prefer them over the electric, for very fundamental reasons: They work even when the electricity goes off, and the secretary can continue, generally, to use the machine without being stranded until the repairman arrives. Secretaries spoiled by the electric machines will vow they are faster — yet the typewriting experts of old got just as much steam out of the manual as today's typists can get out of the electric machines. It takes a little more physical power, and a certain expertise, but once the technique is mastered, the results speak for themselves.

Of course, there is always the possibility that the computer will become so refined that the boss can dictate directly into a computer, with the printed copy produced as rapidly as it is dictated. Then where will that leave the secretary? Do you think the boss will be eager for such computerization? How much change can one generation of businessmen absorb?

Perhaps the secretarial job itself will become vastly different from what it is today. You have learned of the many and varied types of duties a secretary may perform for his boss; the skill area of shorthand and typewriting is but a very small portion of the job. It is conceivable that the skill area may be completely eliminated from the secretarial position, to be replaced by other types of duties and responsibilities. Word-processing centers are already being established. Explore the centers – so similar in nature to the typing pool, but utilizing electronic devices and telephone lines for dictation.

Already some secretaries have stenographers of their own, or access to a word-processing center. They have already begun to function in the capacity of administrative assistants rather than as secretaries. As administrative assistants, they may be responsible for making minor decisions in the absence of the employer, or assume certain minor portions of the boss's job as they are delegated. Certain kinds of correspondence can be handled by them, freeing the boss for more important tasks to be assumed from *his* boss.

It is already being predicted that young people entering the job market will change the type of job they perform at least three times. The initial job may never change, but the classification of duties to be completed may be altered a number of times. This creates the need for flexibility toward change.

It has been said that unless one is flexible, he will become stagnant. Yet, can change be too rapid for the good of society? Should not the students of today prepare to be flexible, yet prepare to use caution in initiating change? Still, the question is, *Why*? *Why* change – what will result? *When*? *When* to change so that the change will be compatible with the rest of life in the society? *How*? *How* to change so that the effects will not be detrimental to other major segments of the economy and, therefore, to society?

As change occurs, the secretary must be prepared for it if he is to be successful. Change of some nature will be with you. If you can bow to change as the willow bends to the forces of the wind, you will survive. If you are inflexible, like the mighty oak, you may have a rough time in life, and may eventually be toppled by the forces of change.

Career opportunities are multitudinous already in today's world. What do they hold in the future? Right now it is enough to contemplate the types of jobs the secretary may look forward to in the immediate future.

CAREER OPPORTUNITIES TODAY

Many exciting things can happen to a secretary in a small business firm in your home town. Look around you – how many different kinds of secretaries are there in your own community? Make a list of the various positions. Start with the school you attend — there are educational secretaries at work. Then look at the doctor's offices and hospitals — there are medical secretaries at work. What about the law offices, construction firms, recreational offices, courts, travel agencies, television and radio stations, art firms, architectural and engineering firms, grocery outlets both wholesale and retail, the fashion industry . . . and on and on the list can grow.

Some of these positions require special skills, particularly in the terminology used. But you know, now, how to master that if you should decide to accept one of the more specialized jobs.

You want to get away from the home town? Well, how about being a secretary for a travel agency? Try to arrange for a test from your local agency and make initial contact with their home office, wherever it may be. Or would you like a job with a government official — say, in your state capital, or even in Washington, D.C.? There are state and federal civil-service examinations that may be taken in order to get an initial rating. Check with your local post office, or write to the Civil Service Commission in your state capital or in Washington. Once the initial rating is established, put your business letter-writing techniques into practice and start a correspondence with officials for whom you would like to work. If your professional skills and knowledge are adequately displayed, you may find yourself in that desired position.

If you do not know the kinds of federal jobs available, consult the Civil Service Commission for a list of secretarial jobs. Not only do congressmen need secretaries, many of their wives need social secretaries. The service agencies of the government, such as the FBI, the Department of Health, Education and Welfare, the U.S. courts, and others need secretaries.

Would you like an overseas job with the government? This can be arranged through the civil-service agency. How about being a secretary to an ambassador, or being attached to an embassy in a foreign country?

Sometimes a private employment agency can be worth the fees the secretary pays to get a job. If you want to move to a large city and you have no contacts there, consider consulting a private employment agency, names of which can be obtained by purchasing a newspaper from that city. Be perfectly honest with them about what you want and how skilled you are, and see what they can do for you before you spend your money for moving expenses. When you receive your answers, evaluate them for honesty and integrity, and if you question, even slightly, the ethics of the response, either drop their service or check them out further.

Many employers in metropolitan areas rely solely on placement agencies. They would rather pay the fees of the secretaries they hire than set up an advertisement and spend the time necessary to screen applicants. A placement agency can screen applicants according to guidelines established by an employer. It is possible to have several interviews scheduled for the first few days after your arrival in a metropolitan area if you contact such an agency in advance. Even if the secretary must pay the fee, it may be well worth it to prevent several weeks of unemployment. A good secretary can almost always find a job wherever he goes, but it may be more difficult to do it alone.

There are temporary employment agencies that can also be helpful — "temporary" meaning that they find only temporary kinds of employment. Such employment may consist of substituting for a secretary on vacation or for one who will be absent for one or two days. There are a number of such agencies in large cities. Again, the purchase of a newspaper published in the desired metropolitan area will give you the names of the agencies. By working at temporary employment, you can have an opportunity to look at a large number of companies and offices, to determine just what the area has to offer and where you might like to accept employment. This method will work best for the secretary with some experience, since it is less difficult for him to adjust to new office situations so that he produces enough work to pay for his hire.

Have you ever thought of going to work for a large company that has overseas interests — such as an oil company? Many opportunities exist in such companies for a change of assignment to an overseas job of limited duration.

Or have you ever thought of simply going into business for yourself? In one city, an enterprising young woman set up a secretarial agency on a large boat. Interested young executives could bring their work to the boat, and they could have a relaxing day in the sun, with a secretary immediately available to complete that needed correspondence or that pesky report. One advantage of such an agency is the peace and quiet that is simply not available in the average business office.

Some secretaries arrange to set up an office at a large hotel or vacation resort. They are available for one letter or many. The guests at such a hotel may dictate directly over the phone, or may be provided an office for temporary use in dictation. This service is particularly appealing to men and women who travel and have numerous reports or letters to prepare even though a personal secretary is not available.

The kind of job you hold will depend upon what you want, the kind of personality you have, and the degree of skill you possess. Only you can determine what happiness you will find in a particular type of job; and you may have to hold several jobs before you settle upon *the one*.

Since it is important for everyone to be happy in the work he does, you should be selective in accepting even your first job. The beginner may take the first job offered because he fears he may not be offered another. This is all right *if* the job is one in which he can be happy. If there are any doubts, however, he should not accept the job. As with any new employee, the secretary must be with the firm several months before becoming efficient enough to earn the salary. For this reason, it is unfair to accept a position you do not feel you can stay with for a fairly long period of time. Having worked in a position for some time, if you find you are not happy in it, by all means start arranging to find another one — but be fair in giving sufficient notice.

There are still people who believe a woman should be relegated to the home and, like children, seen but not heard. In modern society, this outmoded idea is being overcome. Each person, male or female, should do what it makes him happy to do, whether he is black, yellow, red, white, or a mixture of any or all colors. Happiness is an important ingredient of life, and so much time is spent on the job that the quality of that time is precious.

The secretary, or any other jobholder for that matter, must know what he wants. Those who claim discrimination and unfairness in the marketplace should be prepared to back up their demands with cold, hard facts, or they may be suspected of merely trying to get something for nothing. If you are willing to put effort into your job, if you are willing to strive for improvement, and if you are willing to earn your way and then some, you will probably succeed in reaching your goals.

Sometimes, however, such cries are legitimate. Sometimes

society moves too swiftly for the good of all, and one group gets left behind. Sometimes all reasonable efforts to call attention to such a group are ignored, and drastic action seems necessary to achieve change — but this does not happen as frequently as some would have you believe.

Learn to think for yourself. Learn to take appropriate action to help yourself. Learn to be flexible toward change, to learn a new job if need be, to move from one section of the country to another — if necessary, from one part of the world to another, or from one planet to another if that is what it takes. If you learn to think for yourself and determine your own needs, you will be able to direct your own life into the paths of success, however you interpret success.

Success is not the same for all people. Success for me is not necessarily success for you. Do not judge your success by me, or by your parents, or by your friends. Judge your success by what you want in life and what you are willing to do to achieve it.

The opportunities are there — seek and you may find them.

Suggested Projects

Ask a representative of a private employment agency to visit as a guest lecturer to describe how the agency functions.

Arrange a panel of businessmen to discuss jobs of the future — the business world of the future. Emphasize to them that you are interested in the long run — 10-20 years in the future.

Arrange for guest lecturers such as a legal secretary, a medical secretary, an engineering secretary, or other types of secretaries, to discuss the way they see their jobs in the future.

10

The Whole Secretary

10

The Whole
Beekeeper

What is a secretary? You have read this book and you have practiced some of the techniques used by the secretary. Now is the time to sit back in your chair and *think* about all the aspects of the secretarial position. Conjure up in your mind what you now conceive to be the picture of the secretary. Does it differ from the picture you visualized in Chapter 1?

What does it take to be a successful secretary? The secretarial position is exciting — but the successful secretary is realistic, mature, responsible. The successful secretary pays attention to the details of the job as well as to the exciting duties. It is necessary to appear well groomed and confident while attending to the routine office tasks. Thus, a secretary is an actor at times.

The successful secretary is a public-relations expert — with the boss, with fellow workers, and in contacts with the public — maintaining self-control when excited, when bored, when angry, when hurt, when confused. The secretary will make decisions necessary to maintain good human relations and will accept the responsibility for those actions. The professional secretary will assure that the job gets finished even if the boss must be prodded to action.

The successful secretary is the shining light of the office — with a personality that will make the office a more pleasant place for everyone to work. The professional secretary is courteous, friendly, responsive to and understanding of the problems of others, and able to handle awkward situations with ease. An efficient secretary gets the job done, even at the expense of personal whims and desires, by being cooperative, helpful, and understanding.

The successful secretary maintains a loyal attitude to the boss and to the firm, even in times of stress. It is a quiet loyalty, which is expressed through actions rather than words. Loyalty shows through the secretary's perceptiveness to the needs of the boss and to the needs of the office. A professional secretary takes the initiative to see that the routine tasks of the office are completed with as little furor as possible.

A professional secretary is known for grooming techniques that are usually copied by the younger members of the office staff. Young secretaries strive to follow the example of a successful person. A professional secretary understands the need to dress in the style of the times without giving up good taste and individuality, studying the impression given and being flexible toward change when change is appropriate.

The successful secretary has developed good work habits, resulting in efficient and precise production. The professional is seldom caught short, because he is prepared with notes he needs to complete each job.

The successful secretary is able to handle confidential material with ease and grace, so that it is seldom apparent to anyone else that such material is being produced. All material is handled as confidential.

The successful secretary stays up to date and, apparently, always knows the newest terminology used in the business world. The professional secretary is a good reference source – seeming to know where to find answers to questions asked by others. An efficient secretary knows what is new in equipment, usually has some idea of the cost, and can give an opinion on equipment and supplies.

The successful secretary seems capable of talking to any class of people with ease. Conversation never really seems to be difficult. A professional secretary is a good listener when necessary and is able to keep confidences without seeming to be puffed up with confidential information. A professional is well read, tactful in discussions, and diplomatic in stating opinions.

The successful secretary is able to straighten out involved sentences with the ability to select words that interpret a clear message.

The successful secretary is rather a moderate person, not extreme in anything – not extremely shy, not extremely aggressive, not extremely easy to work with nor extremely difficult to work with. He does not claim to know everything; he does claim to know a great deal. The professional is simply not an extremist, but rather a moderate. The professional tries to understand other people and tries to understand himself. The happy secretary is confident, radiant, and eager.

The successful secretary knows about other jobs but is happy in his own, because, of all the positions available, this is the chosen one.

The professional knows what the future can hold, and is confident in making future plans.

Suggested Project

Arrange an "Honor the Professor" day with a coffee. You might even invite a visiting lecturer chosen by the class as outstanding for his contribution to the class during the term, and honor them both. One or two of the class members could present very brief speeches, or you might arrange a little role-playing game in their honor. Wind up the session by serving coffee.

PART TWO

The Professional Secretary's Reference Manual

CONTENTS

TIPS ON SKILL TECHNIQUES

A good secretary will seek the greatest possible utilization of the typewriter. Each typewriter should be accompanied by a manual of operational procedures. If you are not provided such a manual, contact the company that manufactured the machine and request that a manual be provided. Since each company manufactures a number of different models of typewriter, be sure to state the model number and the serial number, so that the proper manual may be sent.

Read the manual thoroughly. Familiarize yourself with the unique features of the machine, as well as the most obvious features. Practice on your machine until you have mastered each of its capabilities. The time spent on practice will pay off in production.

Preparing A Report

There are times when the secretary will type a report to be submitted by his employer. A report, to be properly appreciated and to gain the best recognition possible, should be a thing of beauty.

The preparation of a report is similar to the preparation of a work of art — the beginning stages, the polishing stages, and then the completion of the artwork, with a perfect frame to intensify its beauty. A report begins with a rough draft. The rough draft will go through various stages of polishing, and the final copy is prepared and placed in an appropriate folder to enhance its attractiveness.

During the polishing stages of the rough draft, the secretary may need to type it from three to five times, each time producing a new draft for the purpose of polishing and refining. Each of the drafts should be identified, so they will not be confused with each other, by the words "First Draft," "Second Draft," "Third Draft" (see the illustration) typed at the top of the first page of the draft. Only for the final product should the word "Draft" be removed.

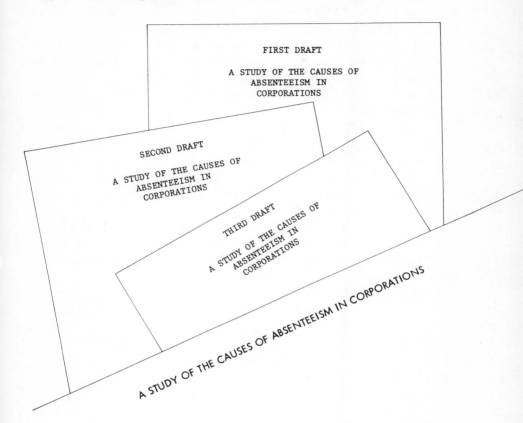

The first draft of a report is the attempt of the writer to put ideas into words. Knowing that there will be great need for revision, the secretary will leave a lot of "white space" by using triple spacing. Nothing is as frustrating to the writer as to be cramped for white space in adding material or changing its formation. A good secretary, to eliminate as much frustration from the job as possible as the various drafts are typed, will judge from the number of changes on the current draft whether to use triple or double spacing. As the revisions diminish, indicating that the draft is taking final form, the secretary can judge the final length of the report when he is able to use double spacing on the rough draft.

During the revision procedure, an alert secretary will check the format for proper style and form. It might be necessary to suggest changes in wording to assure parallelism in the headings. Here the secretary will find a good friend in one of the report-writing manuals to be found in bookstores or in the company policy manual.

The final draft of the report should be double-spaced for ease of reading. The margins should conform to a good report style as outlined in a good reference manual. When every change has been made on the rough draft, the secretary prepares for the final typing of the report.

Before starting the final draft, the secretary should check the typewriter ribbon, to be sure that it will produce the same shading throughout the report regardless of its length. A ribbon change in the middle of the report can result in a poor overall appearance. The use of a ribbon that produces various shadings also spoils the appearance of the report.

If a new ribbon is placed on the machine before the start of the final draft, the type bars may become clogged with ink rather rapidly, and frequent cleaning may be necessary to produce sharp, clear copy throughout the report.

The long and tedious work done by the writer of the report can be either enhanced or ruined by the work of the secretary. The final content of the report is the responsibility of the boss, but the final appearance of the report is the responsibility of the secretary. If both do their work well, they will have a product of which each can be equally proud.

Preparing a Letter

Letters are portraits — of you, your company, your boss. As such a portrait, a letter should represent only the best example of your work. Rules for typing letters can be found in many typewriting books. There are variations, however, that can make your letters stand out from others received at the same time. With each letter you type, strive to make a distinct impression — to draw attention to the main focal point of that letter. If it was important to your boss to dictate the letter, it should be important to you, as a secretary, to focus the attention of the reader on it.

Titles. Titles involve emotions, therefore, it is sometimes difficult to know how to use them. Because they are highly personal,

the use of an incorrect title can be insulting, and if the reader feels even slightly insulted, the impact of the letter is diminished.

If the addressee holds a degree or title, use that designation. In today's business world, many retired military people are entering a second profession. Military titles have no status in business and should be dropped for office use. In personal correspondence, however, these titles may be used, followed by "Ret.," the abbreviation for the word "retired."

When a name is obviously feminine, treat it as such. Women are fairly new to the executive and administrative areas of the business world, and they are frequently insulted by the blanket assumption that anyone in a high-level position must be a man. A secretary will make fewer mistakes if he will think of executives as executives — not as men or women. No businessman wants to insult the person to whom he writes, and part of the duty of the secretary is to help to assure that this does not happen.

Use the exact name of the addressee *as it appears* on business correspondence. The firm name should be written *as it appears* on the letterhead. The purpose of the business letter is to communicate, and the best communication comes when the reader can get to the body of the letter with an open mind.

Emphasis. Use white space to make a point. Creative use of the typewriter to form certain designs has been included in most of the typewriting books, and in some instances may provide a way of drawing special attention to an item. That, combined with your own initiative and creativity, can make your letters distinctive. Overuse of a particular technique should be avoided lest it become an accepted pattern, which would diminish its effectiveness for the purpose for which it was designed.

The general rule of a double space between paragraphs can be followed for most letters. However, if you want to draw attention to a separate series of paragraphs, use four to six spaces between them. White space is very effective when it falls somewhere in the body of the letter.

There are many ways to draw attention to a specific point you wish to emphasize. Become an artist on the typewriter, and be creative in your thinking. This, of course, requires a complete grasp of grammar, punctuation, and basic rules of writing.

Study the following examples and then create some of your own:

The interrupting phrase, non-restrictive, normally set off by a comma.

Example 1-A:

```
    Statements that were . . . by his own admission
. . . intended to discredit the individual should be
eliminated.
```

Example 1-B:

```
    Statements that were (by his own admission) in-
tended to discredit the individual should be elim-
inated.
```

Example 1-C:

```
    Statements that were -- by his own admission --
intended to discredit the individual should be elim-
inated.
```

The listing of items.

Example 2-A:

The suggestion concerning
   . . . the lowering of basic rates
   . . . the increasing of rates for special
       services
   . . . the selection procedures for customers
should be considered at the next administrative session.

Example 2-B:

The suggestion concerning (1) the lowering of basic rates, (2) the increasing of rates for special services, and (3) the selection procedures for customers should be considered at the next administrative session.

Example 2-C:

The suggestion concerning
   1. The lowering of basic rates
   2. The increasing rates for special services
   3. The selection procedures for customers
should be considered at the next administrative session.

Meeting dates and speakers.

Example 3-A:

. . . meeting has been set for
      December 2
      Room 403
      8 p.m.

We have arranged for a special guest speaker, Mr. James J. Jones, who has a professional background in the subject of ecology.

Example 3-B:

. . . meeting has been set for

    December 2
    Room 403
    8 p.m.

We have arranged for a special guest speaker . . . Mr. James J. Jones . . . who has a professional background in the subject of ecology.

Example 3-C:

. . . meeting has been set for . . . December 2, Room 403, 8 p.m. . . . We have arranged for a special guest speaker

    James J. Jones

who has a professional background in the subject of ecology.

Creative techniques combined with the always-proper format of the business letter will focus attention of the reader on the exact information you wish to emphasize. Points to be deemphasized can then be placed in the main text of the letter, thereby diminishing any negative impact.

Preparing a Memorandum

The memorandum is an informal type of communication that is directed between offices within the same company. Memorandum head should be used if it is available; otherwise, the secretary may type the necessary information at the top of the first sheet. Such information should include the name of the addressee, the name of the sender, the date, and the subject. Maintaining the same subject line for all correspondence pertaining to the same item will facilitate filing and retrieval of the correspondence.

Omit personal and corporation titles, but retain professional titles:

```
TO:   Mary Greene
      Thomas White
      Lori Brown, Ed.D.

          or

TO:   Mary Greene
      Thomas White
      Dr. Lori Brown
```

The name and/or title of the writer may be omitted or shown at the bottom of the memo, as preferred by the writer or by company policy.

Initials of the dictator and the stenographer should appear several lines below the text, or name, if used.

Multiple addresses should be shown by typing each name in full on the heading sheet. Names should be listed in order of rank importance — or if the same rank, alphabetically.

The second and succeeding pages of a memo may be handled as follows:

```
LeRoy Anderson, et al.    -2-      February 7, 1973
                          or
Subject: Fiscal Budget    -2-      February 7, 1973
```

Copy routing may be indicated by placing the notation and names flush with the left margin, below the initials of the dictator and stenographer.

```
RG:cd
cc:   Roy Walker
      Jerry Jones
      Ann White
```

Copy routing is sometimes indicated by inclusion on the memo head:

From: Ray Treene   Date: September 28, 1972
To: LeRoy Anderson   Copies: Roy Walker
          John Brown   Jerry Jones
          Dan MacGruder   Ann White
          Roy Carpenter

Subject: Fiscal Budget

Copies are often sent to individuals not listed as receiving copies on the memo head. These are referred to as *blind copies.* The notation "bc:" followed by the name of the individual to receive such a copy should be placed below any other copy notation and should appear *only on the file copy.*

Handling Mail

When the mail is received, the secretary should — with the approval of the boss — open each piece, scan it for content and importance, and place it in priority order. Once again, the folder becomes important. Color coding can be helpful — for example, red for Priority I, blue for Priority II, and green for Priority III. As the mail is taken care of, the folder will be returned to the secretary.

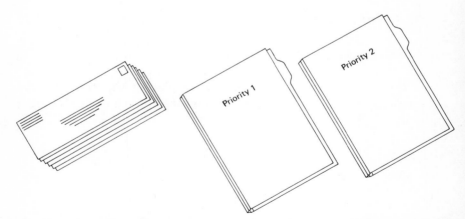

If additional mail is received before the folders are returned to the secretary, it is not necessary to prepare a duplicate set. Simply assign the priorities, take the correspondence into the employer's office, and put it into the proper folder.

Mail should always carry the date and time received. A stamp for this purpose not only allows the employer to identify time of receipt but may prove valuable for later reference. The date stamp should be clearly visible.

Taking Dictation

The secretary will find it helpful to take a file folder to dictation sessions. Each item to which the boss refers can be placed in the folder, providing a compact package with which to work during the transcription of the dictation.

Dictation Folder

A secretary who finds that his employer makes frequent changes in the dictation will do well to utilize only one side of the shorthand pad for dictation, leaving the other column to make insertions and corrections.

The secretary will find that future references to old notes will be made more easily if the dates are recorded on the front of the shorthand pad in the space provided. Later reference is also easier when the secretary places the date of each day's dictation on the page where each day's work begins.

Leaving several blank lines between items of dictation helps in scanning the material quickly when the secretary is asked to check notes or when searching material for instructions. The use of color coding can be effective in identifying items of priority. A quick switch of pens to provide later identification can be most helpful. For example, the boss may dictate several letters and then tell the secretary that the last one should go out before noon. A quick switch to a red pen and a line placed next to the letter, or a quick note written in the column reserved for instructions, will enable the secretary to identify this letter as the important one.

Nothing pleases the employer more than to have his instructions carried out exactly as he has defined them. The use of a particular-color pen to write down instructions that are to be fulfilled will help keep them separated from the ordinary dictation and will assure that the secretary will not overlook even one.

Handling Transcription

When a secretary has completed the correspondence, the material is presented to the boss as a package. Each piece of correspondence has its own envelope attached with a paper clip. The envelope should not obscure the letter or memorandum, since the boss should be able to read the material before affixing his signature.

If instructions have been given to enclose or attach items, these items should be enclosed in the envelope or attached to the letter *before* submitting the material for signature. The boss should see the final package.

When the secretary is faced with a rush job, such as a letter to be out within the hour, the letter should be presented immediately upon completion — it should not be delayed.

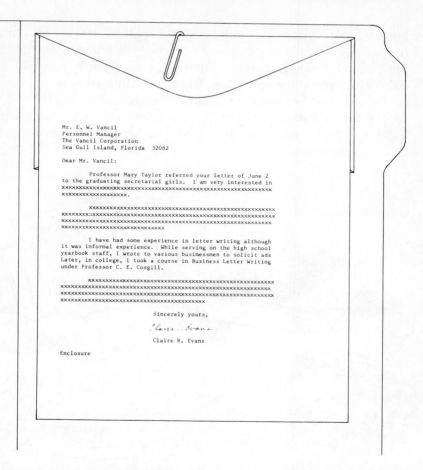

Mr. E. W. Vancil
Personnel Manager
The Vancil Corporation
Sea Gull Island, Florida 32082

Dear Mr. Vancil:

  Professor Mary Taylor referred your letter of June 2
to the graduating secretarial girls. I am very interested in
xxxxxxxxxxxxxxxxxxxxxxxxxxxxxxxxxxxxxxxxxxxxxxxxxxxxxxxxxxxxxx
xxxxxxxxxxxxxxxxxxx.

  xxxxxxxxxxxxxxxxxxxxxxxxxxxxxxxxxxxxxxxxxxxxxxxxxxxxx
xxxxxxxxxxxxxxxxxxxxxxxxxxxxxxxxxxxxxxxxxxxxxxxxxxxxxxxxxxxxxx
xxxxxxxxxxxxxxxxxxxxxxxxxxxxxxxxxxxxxxxxxxxxxxxxxxxxxxxxxxxxxx
xxxxxxxxxxxxxxxxxxxxxxxxxxxxxxx

  I have had some experience in letter writing although
it was informal experience. While serving on the high school
yearbook staff, I wrote to various businessmen to solicit ads
Later, in college, I took a course in Business Letter Writing
under Professor C. E. Cosgill.

  xxxxxxxxxxxxxxxxxxxxxxxxxxxxxxxxxxxxxxxxxxxxxxxxxxxxx
xxxxxxxxxxxxxxxxxxxxxxxxxxxxxxxxxxxxxxxxxxxxxxxxxxxxxxxxxxxxxx
xxxxxxxxxxxxxxxxxxxxxxxxxxxxxxxxxxxxxxxxxxxxxxxxxxxxxxxxxxxxxx
xxxxxxxxxxxxxxxxxxxxxxxxxxxxxxxxxxxxxxxxxxx

      Sincerely yours,

      Claire R. Evans

      Claire R. Evans

Enclosure

Transcription prepared for the employer's signature should be placed in a position that protects its content. The use of correspondence folders has become a popular way of presenting the material to the boss. Such a folder should be different from the regular file folder, so that it can be easily identified. If a regular file folder is used, perhaps the words "For Your Signature" could be printed in color in large letters on the front.

Handling Travel Arrangements

Each company has its own methods of arranging for travel. The secretary should refer to the company policy manual and familiarize himself with the major points of the policy. If the boss travels frequently, it might be necessary to record the telephone numbers of the various airlines, train depots, or car-rental agencies in a convenient place for reference. When you find some helpful person on the other end of the line, obtain his name and record it beside the appropriate telephone number, so that you can make an effort to build a rapport with him that will ease your problems in making travel arrangements.

If the company does not provide specific arrangements with a particular chain of hotels and motels, it might be wise to obtain a "Guide for Travelers" from one or two of the major travel agencies. Such a guide will list the hotels and motels in a given city and will usually provide rates.

Check the company policy manual to determine the extent of insurance coverage for the traveler. If you find nothing to guide you in this matter, consult your employer for the amounts of insurance you may need to obtain for him. The boss is of value to the company, and he should always be covered with insurance in the event of an accident.

FORMS OF ADDRESS

It is very important to good human relations that proper forms of address be used in the preparation of correspondence. Some of the more commonly used forms of addresses are shown below.

The Doctorate

Degrees are correctly written using periods, with no space after periods within the abbreviation. When an executive typewriter with proportional spacing is used, it is acceptable to omit periods:

```
Dr. John Jones
Doctor John Jones
John Jones, Ed.D.
John Jones, PhD
```

If there is a title as well as a degree, both may be used:

```
The Most Reverend John Jones, Ph.D.
```

Only one degree (the highest) should be used after the name, *unless* the degrees are in *different* fields:

```
John Jones, Ph.D., LL.D.
```

Dr. may be used when it precedes a full name; *Doctor* is used when it precedes a surname only.

The Woman

Apply the same form of address as used for men. Check previous correspondence carefully for titles such as doctorates. *Madam* is the corresponding title to *Mr.*:

Madam Secretary   Madam President

When gender is known to be feminine but marital status is unknown, use either *Miss* or *Ms.*

Acting Heads

The word *Acting* precedes the title in the address, but never in the salutation:

```
Mr. John Jones
Acting Mayor of Podunk
Podunk, Illinois

My dear Mayor Jones:
```

Professional Titles

Professional titles — General, Colonel, President, Professor — are written out when used with only the surname. They are usually abbreviated before the full name.

Honorary Titles

Honorary titles — Reverend, Honorable — are written in full if preceded by *the*, and are followed by the given name (or two initials) of the individual:

```
The Honorable Carl Black
The Honorable D.F. Brown
```

or else by another title and the surname:

```
The Reverend Mr. White.
```

The honorary title *The Honorable* is bestowed upon those holding the following offices: The vice-president of the United States, Speaker of the House of Representatives, cabinet officers, U.S. senators, governors and other state officials, mayors, and foreign ministers.

STYLE VARIATIONS

There are variations of letter styles that are unique in the way the parts of the letter are handled. When a style is chosen for use, adhere to it. There are, however, various ways of handling certain features within a letter style. The expert typist will determine when there is a choice. The executive or secretary who lacks a basic knowledge of style has no excuse for poor-quality work. What is not known can be learned through the use of reference manuals and textbooks.

The government or military style is different from the normal business usage. A secretary must adapt to the type of office in which he works and use the style compatible to the desires of the company or the government or military agency.

Dates

In normal business usage, the name of the month is spelled out; figures are used for the day and the year:

```
February 23, 1973
```

The month precedes the day:

```
        I received your letter of February 23.
        The date for the conference is March 1.
```

When the day precedes the month, either spell out the day or use *-st, -d,* or *-th*:

```
We expect an answer by the twenty-third (or 23d) of
        February.
By the first (or 1st) of March we expect to have fur-
        ther information available.
```

When the day is written without the month, either spell out the date for clarity or use *-st, -th,* or *-d*:

```
We expect an answer by the 23d.
May we hear from you by the first?
```

In any case, when a style is chosen, be consistent.

There are several ways of showing dates that are sequential:

```
March 1-15
June 10-July 15
1970-1975
```

The hyphen serves as the word *through.*

In the military style of expressing dates, the day precedes the month:

```
21 April 1972
```

A.D. (in the year of our Lord) and B.C. (before Christ) are typed in capitals, with a period following each letter:

```
A.D. 1972 (A.D. precedes date)
1592 B.C. (B.C. follows date)
```

Attention Line

The attention line is used to direct correspondence to an individual within a firm. The use of the attention line does not change the salutation, *Gentlemen.* A personal title should precede a name in the attention line:

```
VEPRO Consolidated          VEPRO Consolidated
999 Avenue R                999 Avenue R
Washington, D. C.  22201    Washington, D. C.  22201

Attention Mr. Vance         ATTENTION SERVICE CONSULTANT


VEPRO Consolidated          VEPRO Consolidated
999 Avenue R                999 Avenue R
Washington, D. C.  22201    Washington, D. C.  22201

Attention Miss Vance        ATTENTION DOCTOR VANCE
```

Subject and Reference Lines

The subject and reference lines usually accomplish the same purpose. There may be times when both may be used in the same correspondence:

```
Gentlemen:                          Gentlemen:
SUBJECT:   Contract Renewal              Wallace Deed
RE:        John Wallace File


Gentlemen:                          Gentlemen:
Subject:  Wallace Deed                 WALLACE DEED


Gentlemen:                          Gentlemen:
In Re:  Wallace Deed                Reference:  Wallace Deed


Gentlemen:

  File No. 34621
```

Military style places subject and reference lines immediately below the date preceding the inside address:

```
                                   1 June 1972
                        Subject:   Retirement Fund
                        In Re:     C-176-04136
```

Salutation and Complimentary Close

The salutation and complimentary close frame the letter. The way in which they are handled has a psychological effect on the reader. The letter style should be selected carefully to suit the reader, when possible:

```
          The Honorable John Jones
          United States Senate
          Washington, D. C.

          Dear Senator Jones:

            xxxxxxxxxxxxxxxxxxxxxxxxxxxxxx
          xxxxxxxxxxxxxxxxxxxxxxxxxxxxx

                       Sincerely yours,

                       Charles Vance
                       Sales Manager
          eb
```

The Honorable John Jones
United States Senate
Washington, D. C.

xxxxxxxxxxxxxxxxxxxxxxxxxxxxxxxxxxxxxxx
xxxxxxxxxxxxxxxxxxxxxxxxxxxxxxxxxxxxxxx
xxxxxxxxxxxxxxxxxxxxxxxxxxxxxxxxxxxxxxx
xxxxxxxxxxxxxx

Charles Vance - Sales Manager

eb

P.S.   xxxxxxxxxxxxxxxxxxxxxxxxxxxxxxx
xxxxxxxxxxxxxxxxxxxxxxxxxxxxxxxxxxxxx

The Honorable John Jones
Mayor of Alexandria
Alexandria, Virginia   22311

Dear Sir:

xxxxxxxxxxxxxxxxxxxxxxxxxxxxxxxxxxxxxx
xxxxxxxxxxxxxxxxxxxxxxxxxxx

Very truly yours,

Charles Vance
Sales Manager

eb

Enclosure

Mr. John Jones, Ph.D.
Principal, Hammond High School
Alexandria, Virginia   22311

Dear Doctor Jones:

xxxxxxxxxxxxxxxxxxxxxxxxxxxxxxxxxx
xxxxxxxxxxxxxxxxxxxxxxxxxxxxxxxxxxxxx

                    Sincerely yours,

                    VEPRO CONSOLIDATED

                    Charles Vance,
                    Sales Manager

eb

Mailing Notations

A mailing notation — airmail, special delivery, registered — if necessary or desired on the original letter, may be placed on the line directly below the initials or enclosure notation.

On the envelope, the mailing notation is typed above the address in capital letters. It may be underscored for special attention.

Postscript — P.S.

A postscript is an afterthought — which is pertinent but does not require that the letter be retyped to include the information. A postscript is typed following every part of the business letter as it currently exists. If the letter indicates enclosures, then the postscript will follow the enclosure notations. If, however, the enclosures are mentioned in the postscript — then the enclosure notation will follow the postscript. A postscript may be introduced with "P.S.," or may be simply typed in the appropriate place with no introduction. In such case, the format of the postscript will parallel that of the letter.

NUMBERS

In the business world, numbers are usually of such significance that they should be handled in figures for easy identification:

Of the 30 executives, 10 were selected to head up a new branch office.

The unemployment rate rose .5% during the month of June.

The general rule for numbers falling in text material is that numbers containing less than three digits are spelled out; numerals are used for numbers containing three or more digits. Whether this rule is followed depends on the importance of the numbers cited:

A supply requisition must be filled out completely, three copies to be sent to Purchasing. Quantity must be clearly designated; i.e., ten cartons, six gross, seven boxes. The description of the item ordered should be as complete as possible.

A supply requisition must be filled out completely, 3 copies to be sent to Purchasing. Quantity must be clearly designated; i.e., 10 cartons, 6 gross, 7 boxes. The description of the item ordered should be as complete as possible.

When using a mixture of numbers, use Arabic numerals:

Of the 395 students in the graduating class, 9 were summa cum laude, 27 were magna cum laude, and 48 were cum laude.

Technical or statistical explanations use Arabic numerals:

Since a 5-bit word would only allow 32 (which is 2x2x2x2x2) distinct interpretations, it is clear that at least 6 bits are necessary to provide for the 26 letters and 10 digits.

Percentages, decimals, and dates are expressed in numbers:

Composite of key indicators of future economic activity fell in September to 113.4% of the 1967 average from a downward-revised 114.6% in August.

Numerals are used to express numbers combined with abbreviations and to express dates:

Educ. 10 will be offered during the Winter Quarter.

The showing, worse than the analysts predicted, indicates the strike that began Sept. 14 is hurting the auto maker more than expected. /Spell out the month unless space is extremely limited./

Exact sums of money should be expressed in numerals:

In Chicago, for example, prices fell $10, to
$41.05 a ton for a key grade.

Street addresses and telephone numbers are expressed in
numerals. Spell out numerical street names when they form one
word; otherwise, use figures.

The office is located at 2456 Fourth Street;
the telephone number is CO3-9771.

Compass points appearing in street names should be spelled out:

3097 West Jefferson Street

but compass points representing sections of a city should be
abbreviated:

3097 Jefferson Street, N.W.

Ordinals and fractions should be spelled out, except when the
fraction is part of a three-digit or larger number.

On the test, one-tenth of the students
scored eighty, which represented 120 1/2
correct answers.

The use of numerals to express one set of figures avoids
confusion when a series of figures is necessary.

On the test, eighty-two made 1-2 errors;
sixty-four made 3-4 errors.

Use numerals to express the time of day when it is combined
with a.m. or p.m.:

The meeting was called for three o'clock;
Mr. Jones left the office at 2:45 p.m.

Never begin a sentence with a numeral:

Thirty days has September.
September has 30 days.

Preliminary pages – Dedication, Preface, Table of Contents – use lowercase roman numerals:

pp. ii, iii, iv

Chapter divisions or volumes use capital roman numerals:

Chapter I, Vol. II

Pages use arabic numerals:

Page 348

For unusual symbols or lettering (such as used in engineering, mathematics, medicine), contact the machine manufacturer for special-key installation on the typewriter.

CAPITALIZATION

Most of the rules for capitalization are commonplace to the secretary or stenographer and need not be repeated here. If needed, they can be found in grammar textbooks, business English textbooks, or other types of reference books.

Several confusing aspects of the use of capitals are shown for quick reference.

Capitalize the shortened name of a government body if it is generally recognized:

The bill passed the House (House of Representatives).

or if the full name has already been used.

Capitalize names of specific geographic locations:

```
Mississippi River
Sun Valley
Chesapeake Bay
Mount Rainier
Big Bend Park
```

The word *city* is capitalized *only* when it is part of the corporate name:

```
Dodge City
```

The word *state* is capitalized *only* when it follows the name of a state:

```
Kansas State
```

ABBREVIATIONS

Some organization names are customarily abbreviated. Such abbreviated forms allow more immediate recognition of the organization than would the names spelled in full: NASA is more rapidly recognized than is the National Aeronautics and Space Administration. HEW is easily recognized as the Department of Health, Education, and Welfare.

ABC   ABC-TV   COMA-FM

Although abbreviations are becoming a way of life, they should be used with care. Too many abbreviations detract from the impact

or tone of the correspondence. Ordinary words should never be abbreviated.

A good dictionary will suffice to check most abbreviations needed in the business world, although it may be desirable to obtain technical manuals for specific areas such as data processing, medicine, law, or education. If large numbers of abbreviations are used, it is suggested that the *Style Manual* and the *United States Government Organization Manual* from the U.S. Government Printing Office be obtained.

The Postal Service is stressing the abbreviations of states, districts, and territories of the United States with the ZIP codes in order to facilitate mail delivery. These abbreviations should be used *only* on the envelope, with the state names spelled in full in the inside address. The following two-letter abbreviations are designated by the Postal Service:

Alabama	AL	Montana	MT
Alaska	AK	Nebraska	NE
Arizona	AZ	Nevada	NV
Arkansas	AR	New Hampshire	NH
California	CA	New Jersey	NJ
Canal Zone	CZ	New Mexico	NM
Colorado	CO	New York	NY
Connecticut	CT	North Carolina	NC
Delaware	DE	North Dakota	ND
District of Columbia	DC	Ohio	OH
Florida	FL	Oklahoma	OK
Georgia	GA	Oregon	OR
Guam	GU	Pennsylvania	PA
Hawaii	HI	Puerto Rico	PR
Idaho	ID	Rhode Island	RI
Illinois	IL	South Carolina	SC
Indiana	IN	South Dakota	SD
Iowa	IA	Tennessee	TN
Kansas	KS	Texas	TX
Kentucky	KY	Utah	UT
Louisiana	LA	Vermont	VT
Maine	ME	Virginia	VA
Maryland	MD	Virgin Islands	VI
Massachusetts	MA	Washington	WA
Michigan	MI	West Virginia	WV
Minnesota	MN	Wisconsin	WI
Mississippi	MS	Wyoming	WY
Missouri	MO		

WORD DIVISION

How each line ends controls, to a large extent, the ease with which the reader follows the thought expressed. Therefore, word division should be based on logic and kept to a minimum. Divide for readability. In each example given, the diagonal (/) shows the point of division:

```
Ellensburg,/Washington   98926
Prof. Ed/Smith
June 17,/1972
```

One-Letter Syllables

When two one-letter syllables occur together within a word, divide between them:

```
gradu/ation
```

When a single-letter syllable occurs within a word, divide after the syllable:

```
tabu/late
```

unless the syllable following contains only two letters (more than two letters are necessary to be carried forward to the new line):

```
read/ily
```

or unless the single-letter syllables *a, i,* or *u* are followed by *-ble, -bly, -cle, -cal,* in which case both syllables should be carried forward to a new line:

```
cler/ical
```

A hyphenated word should be divided *only* at the hyphen:

```
self-/employed
```

When a compound word is written without a hyphen, divide between the words forming the compound:

```
business/men
```

When a final consonant preceded by a single vowel (get) is doubled before adding a suffix (getting), divide between the two consonants:

```
get/ting
```

When a word ends in a double consonant (will), divide between the root word and the suffix:

```
will/ing
```

The word endings *-cial, -tial, -cion, -sion, -tion, -sive, -tive* should be kept as separate units.

```
direc/tion
```

Contractions.
One-syllable words.
Figures or abbreviations.
Words of five or fewer letters.
The last word on two consecutive lines
The last word in a paragraph or on a page.
After a one-letter syllable beginning a word.

For additional help with spelling and word division, reference books such as *20,000 Words*, published by McGraw-Hill Book

Company, or *10,000 Words*, published by the U.S. Government Printing Office, are available.

TABLE FORMATS

A table is used to illustrate data clearly for the reader. Material used in a table usually does not lend itself to narrative form. Arrangement of such material is important for clarity and accurate interpretation. Spacing, lining, arrangement of headings, period leaders, and table placement all contribute to the usefulness of a table.

A table should follow as closely as possible the first mention of it. A short table should be presented in one piece, so it may be necessary to place it on the page following its first mention. If the table is long, one that will take more than one page to complete, it should be started immediately after the first mention.

If a large number of tables are typed by the secretary, it is suggested that a report writer's manual be obtained for greater detail in handling various types of tables.

Sample tables are shown as follows:

TABLE 1

DISTRIBUTION OF
TEST SCORES

Range and Scores	Frequency
79-75	1
74-70	2
69-65	6
64-60	5
59-55	16
54-50	11
49-45	2
44-40	5
39-35	2

Table 1 is unruled because it consists of two columns and is not confusing to the reader.

TABLE 2

FLIGHT FROM NEW YORK
TO EUROPE

Duration	Our Fare	Everyone Else	Savings
Under 14 days	$259*	$570.40	$311.40
14-28 days	259*	393.00	134.00
29-45 days	259*	327.00	68.00
Over 45 days	430	570.40	140.40

*Effective May 15, 1970; slightly higher weekends.

Table 2 is unruled because it is not a difficult table to read, particularly since it contains leader lines to aid the reader. If the width of the table interferes with the text, making the table seem too much a part of the text, it could be boxed by drawing lines around the entire table content.

CONFUSING WORDS

English, like other languages, is full of words that are confusing to one who has not mastered it. To say that the language is confusing is begging the issue. There is no disgrace in the use of a dictionary. A vocabulary becomes much more extensive when a dictionary is used with some consistency. A dictionary should occupy a place of prominence on the desk of any secretary, and it should be *well used.*

Some words, however, give more trouble in daily usage than do others. For that reason, a quick reference is given to some of the more confusing words a secretary may encounter:

Ascent — act of rising
Assent — (noun or verb) consent

> His ascent from trainee to manager was fairly rapid.
> Mr. Brown said that he would assent to the request.

Adherence — attachment
Adherents — followers

> The experiment showed strong adherence between the two pieces of cloth.
> There are many adherents of that philosophy.

Allusion — indirect reference
Illusion — error of vision
Elusion — adroit escape

> An allusion was made to the incident.
> A mirage is an illusion.
> Elusion from a trained investigator is difficult.

Accept — to receive
Except — (verb) to exclude; (preposition) excluding

> Miss Jones will accept the reward for her brother.
> All the brochures are ready except this one.

Adapt — to conform
Adept — skillful
Adopt — to take

> You will soon adapt to the office environment.
> The secretary is adept at her job.
> We will adopt the new policy shortly.

Advice — counsel
Advise — to give counsel

> The advice was questionable.
> He will advise us of proper procedures.

Affect — to act upon
Effect — (verb) to bring about; (noun) result

> How will the change affect his plans?
> This change will effect other changes.
> This change is the direct effect of his decision.

Appraise — to evaluate
Apprise — to inform

> He will appraise the action in terms of the result.
> He will apprise you of his decision tomorrow.

Biannual — twice a year
Biennial — every two years

> Inventory is taken on a biannual basis.
> This is a biennial report.

Canvas — cloth
Canvass — (verb) to solicit; (noun) solicitation, survey

> The sails are made of canvas.
> He will canvass the neighborhood to determine a position on the question.

Capital — (adjective) principal; (noun) seat of government
Capitol — building, statehouse

> The capital will be put up by the banking industry.
> Albany is the capital of New York.
> The capitol needs some renovation.

Complement — what completes a thing
Compliment — (noun or verb) praise

> The office has its complement of workers.
> Mr. Brown will rarely compliment anyone.

Council — assembly
Counsel — (noun) advice given as result of consultation; (verb) to give guidance

> The executives of the firm will meet in council to make a decision.
> They need the counsel of the company attorney.
> The attorney will be asked to counsel them.

Correspondence — letters
Correspondents — those who write letters

> The need for office correspondence has become so great that a new job classification of correspondents has become necessary.

Deference — respect
Difference — dissimilarity

> Deference was given the request of the president.
> The difference of opinion was slight.

Discreet — tactful
Discrete — separate

> He was discreet in the way he handled the disagreement.
> This form is for discrete distribution.

Elicit — to draw forth
Illicit — unlawful

> He should be able to elicit more information.
> The action was illicit.

Eminent — prominent
Imminent — impending

> He comes from an eminent family.
> His election is imminent.

Faze — to disturb
Phase — state of development

> Her actions did not faze him.
> We are entering a new phase of growth.

Farther — more distant
Further — (adj.) more advanced; (verb) to advance

> He was farther from the city than he realized.
> Further advice is needed.
> He can further his career by obtaining additional education.

Holey — full of holes
Wholly — entirely

> The entire argument was holey.
> That statement is not wholly true.

Hypercritical — overcritical
Hypocritical — pretending virtue

> He was hypercritical of his own abilities.
> His attitude is hypocritical; he does not practice what he advocates.

Instants — short periods of time
Instance — example

> The actions were separated by instants.
> One instance of that is shown on this form.

Personal — private
Personnel — staff

> That decision is his personal concern.
> All personnel should be interested in the decision.

Principal — chief, capital
Principle — rule

> The principal idea of an efficiency study is to reveal weaknesses.
> The principle underlying efficiency is adequate planning.

Their — belonging to them
There — in that place
They're — they are

> Their idea was shared by others.
> Place the adding machine over there.
> They're pleased with changes in the office.

To — (preposition)
Too — also
Two — sum of one and one

> Let's move the desk to this spot.
> That's a good idea, too.
> Can we put the two ideas together to get a consensus?

PUNCTUATION

Punctuation is important to the correct transmittal of a thought. It provides for clarity of ideas through conciseness of meaning. Misplaced punctuation can be costly in terms of poor communication, which, in turn, can affect the financial situation of the business firm. A good basic knowledge of the rules of punctuation is the best guarantee of good communication. Most of the information needed can be found in business English or English grammar textbooks. Since business letters should be as nearly error-free as possible, a good reference book should be on the secretary's desk. Infrequently used punctuation marks are illustrated below for quick reference.

Apostrophe

Use the apostrophe for single quotation marks:

```
He responded, "Remember, Theodore Roosevelt said,
'Walk softly and carry a big stick.'"
```

*   **Asterisk**

Use the asterisk to refer the reader to a footnote in a very short manuscript or in a table. Series of asterisks should be avoided. When more than one footnote is indicated, numbers should be used in text material. Tables containing more than one footnote should use small arabic letters.

                                              Brace

Use the brace to join related material. The brace can be made with a ballpoint pen or may be shown by the use of parentheses:

```
Jennifer J. Smith,          )    Chapters
                Plaintiff )        2
                                   3  Personnel
           v.             : OR     5  Manual
Samuel M. Smith,          )        7
                Defendant )        3
                                   4  Correspondence
                                   5  Manual
                                   9
```

$$\underline{/}\underline{/}$$

Brackets

Brackets have been added to many typewriter keyboards. If they do not appear on the keyboard, they may be inserted in ink after the typed copy has been completed. The term "bracket" is sometimes applied also to the parenthesis and the brace. The bracket is used to enclose any part of the text. A few illustrations appear below.

Combined with parenthetical expressions:

/See <u>Standard World Dictionary</u> (Text edition)./

or

(See <u>Standard World Dictionary</u> /Text edition/.)

Introducing comments for clarification:

/According to 1970 census. --Ed./

Phonetic aids to pronunciation:

Braille /brāl/ will be demonstrated to the volunteers.

Interpolation to assure the reader that spelling or logic was faulty in the original quotation:

". . . emmence /sic/ numbers. . . . "
(<u>Sic</u> is always italicized or underscored.)

"Montague Collet was a Norse /English/ financier."

To set off expressions that will assist the reader:

```
/Refer to Table 2, page 27./
```

To indicate that the writer desires to emphasize a point by use of italics not used in the original:

```
"Items may or may not /italics mine/ be numbered."
```

—

Dash

The dash is probably the most misused mark of punctuation, usually because it is confused with the hyphen. Technically, a hyphen is a short, horizontal, straight bar; a dash is of greater length, but the same design. The dash is used to indicate an interruption in thought, whereas the hyphen is used to connect elements of words or word division. The dash is typed by placing two hyphens together with no space in between:

```
. . . likely--although . . .
```

Sometimes it is typed by placing a space before and after one hyphen:

```
. . . likely - although . . .
```

It is *never* typed as a hyphen only:

```
. . . likely-although . . . /Incorrect/
```

The dash is used to indicate an abrupt change of thought within a sentence:

```
It seems likely--although it is a little early to
judge--that he will succeed.
```

When a parenthetical expression contains punctuation, dashes are preferable to parentheses:

```
During our busy season--June, July, August--we
hire students.
```

When an appositive falls at the end of the sentence, it should be separated from the word or expression it explains by a dash:

```
There are two applicants--Jane Smith and Ralph
Green.
The situation wound up in a mess--completely
chaotic!
```

To indicate authorship:

```
A gentleman of our day is one who has money enough
to do what every fool would do if he could afford
it: that is, consume without producing.
                                    --G. B. Shaw
```

For emphasis:

```
An ad in the Post--150,000 subscribers--should be
considered.
```

To show a change in thought:

```
I think we should discuss--no, I believe first we
should consider . . .
```

–   **Hyphen**

A hyphen is used to join a prefix to a capitalized word:

```
        Such thinking is anti-American.
```

A hyphen is used to join prefixes *ex-, self-, quasi-*:

```
        He is an ex-employee.
        Self-control is very important.
        She is quasi-intellectual.
```

A hyphen is used when several words precede and describe a noun. If the words follow the noun, the hyphen is not used:

```
        The well-known author lectured.
        The author was well known.
```

```
      The up-to-date material was used.
      The material used was up to date.
```

Elements of special titles are joined by a hyphen:

```
She is president-elect of National Secretaries.
The ex-congressman will speak.
```

Compounds formed by rhyming or contrasting terms are joined by a hyphen:

```
The pitter-patter of the rain is distracting.
The walkie-talkie is to be used in the field.
```

A hyphen should join the elements of an expression when a single capital letter is the first element:

```
The H-bomb is extremely powerful.
The X-ray picture should reveal if any bones are
broken.
```

/ **Diagonal**

The diagonal is used to abbreviate certain business terms:

```
Refer to B/L No. 43.  /bill of lading/
Send the letter c/o Bill Jones.
The invoice indicates 10/20, n/30.
These pins sell for $1.35/M.  /per thousand/
The serial number on the machine is 3f/876423.
```

The diagonal is used for constructing fractions not supplied on the keyboard of a typewriter. If more than one fraction is written, they should all conform — either they appear on the typewriter, or they are constructed by using the diagonal:

```
He said 6½ gross are under the counter.
His hat size is 6 7/8, but the largest I can
find is 6 1/2.
```

Use the diagonal to indicate an interchange of ideas:

```
Mary and/or Jane will man the switchboard.
```

. . .   or   * * *   **Ellipsis**

An ellipsis (also called *eclipsis*) is used to indicate the ommission of a word or words necessary for the grammatical construction of a sentence, but not required for the understanding of it.

Within a sentence, use three periods separated before, between, and after by one space:

```
Figures are effective because . . . the ease with
which they can be read.
```

At the beginning of a sentence, use three periods with a space before and after each period. The first word is capitalized *only* if you pick up at the beginning of a sentence:

```
. . . the ease with which figures can be read.
```

At the end of a sentence, use four periods, but only if the preceding material forms a complete sentence. The first period indicates the end of the sentence and the last three indicate the ellipsis:

```
Figures are effective because of the ease with
which they can be read. . . .
```

Three spaced asterisks are used to indicate an omission of one or more paragraphs in quoted material and are placed on a line by themselves, either centered or at the point where the paragraph would begin:

```
Figures are effective because of the ease with
which they can be read. . . .

    * * *

The various arguments--advanced in grammar
books--indicate that figures of less than . . .
```

()   **Parentheses**

Parentheses are used to insert a word, phrase, or clause in a sentence that is grammatically correct without the insertion. The parentheses may be used to add variety to the use of commas and dashes:

```
The price ($150) is exorbitant!
The price--$150--is exorbitant!
The price, $150, is exorbitant!
```

When the parentheses appear at the end of the sentence, the period follows:

```
The price is exorbitant (in my opinion).
```

If parenthetical expressions are used within a parentheses, brackets and parentheses may be used interchangeably as shown below.

```
The various arguments--advanced by Keynesian
economists (including the current ones /Newsweek
(November 1970)/)--show basic agreement on but
one point.
```

If the statement within the parentheses will stand alone, the period follows within the parentheses:

```
(Refer to Table 3, p. 18.)
```

```
He read the report. (The report is the one pre-
pared by the special committee on the data-
processing problems. It was prepared, at his
request, last week.) He then asked to have it
duplicated to present to the home office.
```

If a question is asked by the context of the message within the parentheses, the question mark follows inside:

```
I told Mr. Brown (is he the president?) that you
could attend the meeting tommorrow.
```

If the question asked is within the sentence, the question mark follows the parentheses:

```
Can you attend the meeting called for tommorrow by
Mr. Brown (the president)?
```

When an exclamation point is used, the same rule applies as for the question mark:

```
I told him that the decision was to be made to-
morrow (it must be made!).
```

```
The decision (although you may not like it) stands!
```

Commas, semicolons, and colons follow the parentheses:

```
According to Miss Jones (the president's secre-
tary), the decision will be made tomorrow.
```

```
The decision will be made soon (tomorrow); it will
then become standard operating procedure.
```

```
The decision will include the following (accord-
ing to Miss Jones): the number of telephones
needed, the way the phones will be answered, and
the method of referring calls.
```

It is sometimes desirable to use parentheses to clarify amounts of money. This duplication of money amounts also ensures accuracy should there be opportunity for doubt.

```
The increase in technical costs amounts to three
hundred dollars ($300) per month.
```

Parentheses may be used to draw attention by enumerating specific items.

```
He agreed to consider (1) the number of tele-
phones needed, (2) the way the phones should be
answered, and (3) the method of referring calls.
```

```
                    " (When NOT to use)      Quotation Marks
```

When a quotation *exceeds* three (3) typewritten lines, it should be set in from each margin, single-spaced, with no quotation marks.

In typing scripts for theatrical productions and in typing court testimony, quotation marks are unnecessary.

Indirect quotations do not require quotation marks.

Teletypewriter

The Teletypewriter[1] sends electrical impulses over telephone lines, causing simultaneous reproduction of a message in typewritten form on a machine in another office — far or near. The Teletypewriter can operate at 100 words per minute.

Telegraphy

Telegraphic messages are sent exactly as typewritten; therefore, they should be checked carefully before being delivered to the operator. Such messages should be typed on special forms, in all capital letters, double-spaced text. Avoid asterisks, question marks, and parentheses wherever possible, as these symbols do not appear on the machines and must be spelled out by the operator. Use abbreviations, but be sure the message is clear.

TELEX — standard transmission rate of 66 wpm. TELEX is a Western Union service identical to TWX where companies are so equipped. This service may be used for message delivery (TelTex) where the receiver does not have TELEX service. The subscriber pays only for the exact number of seconds spent in communication.

Western Union Telegram. The telegram should be used only when faster methods cannot meet the need. It is the most expensive of the telegraphic services.

TWX (Telephone Wire Exchange Service) — standard transmission rate 60–100 wpm. TWX, formerly a telephone-company machine, is now a Western Union Telegraph Company machine with a direct connection to other companies using this service.[2] The teletype operator contacts another teletype operator by using a TWX number. The charge is logged by the minute, with a three-minute minimum charge. Since Western Union has taken over this service, an expansion in service has made it possible for the TWX operator to dial into a computer to send messages to TELEX machines by using a certain format. It is also possible for the TWX or the TELEX

---

[1] Teletypewriter is a Copyrighted name.
[2] (Western Union purchased this service within the last year)

operator to send messages through the telegraph system without having to go through the telegraph office.

The expansion has also made it possible for both TWX and TELEX to send Mail-Grams through the Post Office. By filing a Mail-Gram (up to 100 words) by 7 p.m., the operator can be assured that the message will be delivered by mail the following morning. The service is cheaper than either the night letter or the telegram.

Telephone

Local.   Local numbers can be determined by referring to the local telephone directory. Numbers most frequently used should be listed in a desk directory for easy reference.

Long Distance.   A *person-to-person* call is placed to a particular individual. The charge begins only when that party is connected with the caller. A *station-to-station* call is placed when information may be obtained from someone in a particular place without necessitating contact with a special individual. It is less expensive than the person-to-person call.

WATS (Wide Area Telephone Service).   When WATS service is available, any number in the WATS area may be called by using the line set aside for WATS service. When large numbers of otherwise long-distance calls are made, the WATS-line installation lessens the cost of such calls to the company for a flat monthly charge.

COPYING AND DUPLICATING SERVICES

Office-management experts estimate that copying accounts for about 40 percent of the typing time in most offices. Copying makes possible mass reproduction of a form, a letter, or a report that formerly had to be typed to obtain a second copy. There are numerous methods of reproducing copy, and attention should be given to both *quality requirements* and *cost incurrence*.

Copying

Six basic methods of copy processes should be consulted to find the best one for a particular job.

Diffusion Transfer. This process is sometimes referred to as *photocopy.* It is not the fastest copy process, and it does require an operator who knows how to use the equipment efficiently and economically. It produces copy with good contrast and can copy all colors.

Dye Transfer. This process is sometimes called the *gelatin transfer process.* During the process of copying, a soft dye is transferred from a master negative to the copy paper. A single master negative can make six or seven copies in rapid succession. As the master dries, it becomes more difficult to transfer the dye. It can copy all colors.

Diazo. This process cannot be used to copy two-sided originals. Such materials must be converted to one-sided originals on some other copying process before the diazo process can be used. The manufacturers for this process claim the lowest cost per copy. Copies can be reproduced in color except for those colors that are transparent to ultraviolet light (some blues and purples).

Stabilization. This process results in a negative that may be stored indefinitely and can be used to make as many copies as desired. It can be used to reproduce photographs and can reproduce copy in almost any color. The process is fairly slow. Copies may gradually deteriorate.

Thermography. This process is sometimes called *infrared* or *heat transfer* copying. Copies are produced in a matter of seconds. This process copies only inks that contain carbon black or a metallic compound. Copies are made on treated paper that may darken if exposed to heat, and they tend to become brittle with age.

Electrostatic. This process uses opposite electrical charges to reproduce the copy. It can copy all colors on ordinary untreated paper. It copies photographs and material containing large solid areas.

Duplicating

Duplicating processes require the preparation of a master, a stencil, or a mat from which the copies are made. This master copy can be filed and the data can be processed again at a future date.

Three basic methods of duplicating processes should be consulted to find the best one for a particular job.

Stencil.   This ink process is often referred to as a *mimeograph* or *Gestetner* process. The stencil may be prepared on the typewriter, or it may be prepared by writing or drawing on the stencil with a stylus or fine ballpoint pen. These stencils can also be prepared with the use of an office copier and a special electronic stencil. The heat of the copier can scan the original and cut the stencil at the same time. These stencils can all be stored and reused. A stencil will usually produce as high as 15,000 copies.

Spirit.   This process is also called *liquid duplicating.* The master uses a special hectograph carbon sheet and is prepared by typing or drawing with a ballpoint pen. The master can be prepared in various colors by changing the color of carbon during preparation. They can be stored and reused. One master can produce from 300 to 450 copies.

Offset.   Offset mats are prepared by typing or by writing or drawing with a special pencil. Metal plates are also available for preparing material containing photographs and other illustrations. Material can be produced in color by changing the ink and rerunning the paper for each color used. The mats can be stored and reused, with approximately 4,000–5,000 copies being produced from each long-run paper mat. The quality of reproduction is high, with the look of "printed" copy.

Each time a project is planned, the planning should include the method of duplication or copying, in order to achieve the desired quality at the lowest possible cost.

Index